FABER

SFC24896

© 2014 by Julia Winterson and Paul Harris
First published in 2014 by Faber Music Ltd and Peters Edition Ltd, London.
All rights administered worldwide by Faber Music Ltd and Peters Edition Ltd, London.

EAN: 978-0-571-53633-7
ISBN10: 0-571-53633-6
FP: 3002

Cover artwork by Dominic Brookman
Music processed by MusicSet 2000
Design by Susan Clarke
Printed in England by Caligraving Ltd

Peters Edition Limited
2–6 Baches Street
London N1 6DN

Faber Music Ltd
Bloomsbury House
74–77 Great Russell Street
London WC1B 3DA

To buy Edition Peters publications or to find out about the full range of titles available
please contact your local music retailer or Edition Peters sales enquiries:
Tel: +44 (0)20 7553 4000   Fax: +44 (0)20 7490 4921
E-mail: sales@editionpeters.com   Website: www.editionpeters.com

To buy Faber Music publications or to find out about the full range of titles available
please contact your local music retailer or Faber Music sales enquiries:
Tel: +44 (0)1279 828982   Fax: +44 (0)1279 828983
E-mail: sales@fabermusic.com   Website: fabermusicstore.com

Introduction

Music is written down so that it can be shared and saved: it enables others to perform your music and is a useful design tool in song-writing, transcribing and arranging. The ability to read music and understand music theory is an enormous asset that opens up many new possibilities for you as a musician.

This music theory book is the first of its kind to cater for the specific needs of rock and pop musicians. Assuming no prior knowledge of music notation, it takes you step by step through rhythm, pitch, scales and modes, chords and forms, and explains terms and signs in simple language. You will learn how to use conventional staff notation in the context of rock and pop music; how to read and write a musical score using TAB and drum notation; and how to use music theory in practical ways to enhance your musical life.

Rock & Pop Theory: The Essential Guide will help you acquire an appropriate rock music vocabulary and an essential overview of the principal rock and pop styles, from the beginning of the twentieth century right through to the present day.

Julia Winterson, September 2014

Acknowledgements

I am grateful to Barry Russell for his help and advice on all things musical and to Marc Layton-Bennett for his drum expertise. My thanks are also due to the music technology and pop students at the University of Huddersfield.

Julia Winterson

Contents

Rhythm

'Rhythm is everywhere. Rhythm has existed since before man evolved: it is an elemental force. There's the rhythm of life: our heartbeat, our pulse, breathing, walking along at a steady pace. The rhythm of nature: night and day, time itself. The rhythm of words: speech and poetry. The rhythm of the modern world: machinery, transport, a clock ticking. Rhythm is all about repetitive patterns of sound or movement; it is, in fact, the heartbeat of music. It includes pulse, relative length of notes, a sense of emphasis, and the general sense of motion that causes music (and life) to move forward.'

Paul Harris

Notes and rests

The word 'rhythm' describes the way that sounds are grouped together in different patterns over time. These patterns are produced by **notes** (sounds) and **rests** (silences) of different lengths. Musical notation is used to represent sounds as notes written on a staff or stave (see page 18). While the *position* of a note on the stave shows its **pitch** (see page 17), the *shape* of the note shows its **duration** – the length of time it lasts in relation to other notes. **Rests** are used to represent silence.

longer duration

British name	American name	Note	Rest
Semibreve	Whole note	o	▬
Minim	Half note	♩ or P	▬
Crotchet	Quarter note	♩ or P	𝄽
Quaver	Eighth note	♪ or ♭	𝄾
Semiquaver	Sixteenth note	♪ or ♭	𝄿
Demisemiquaver	Thirty-second note	♪ or ♭	𝅀

shorter duration

Two notes that are found less frequently are the **breve** or **double whole note** ⫴ (or ═) and the **hemidemisemiquaver** or **sixty-fourth note** ♪.

Semibreve and minim rests look similar: the minim rest sits above the line and the semibreve rest hangs below the line. It might help to think that the minim rest is floating (because it is smaller) and the semibreve rest has sunk (because it is bigger).

British name		American name
1 semibreve	𝅝	1 whole note
= 2 minims	𝅗𝅥	= 2 half notes
= 4 crotchets	𝅘𝅥	= 4 quarter notes
= 8 quavers	𝅘𝅥𝅮	= 8 eighth notes
= 16 semiquavers	𝅘𝅥𝅯	= 16 sixteenth notes
= 32 demisemiquavers	𝅘𝅥𝅰	= 32 thirty-second notes

The relative durations of note-values

Dotted notes

The duration of notes and rests can be lengthened by adding dots.
A single dot placed after a note or rest adds half again to its original value:

Notes

♪. = ♪ + ♪

♩. = ♩ + ♪

𝅗𝅥. = 𝅗𝅥 + ♩

𝅝. = 𝅝 + 𝅗𝅥

o· = o + 𝅗𝅥

Rests

𝄿· = 𝄿 + 𝄿

𝄾· = 𝄾 + 𝄿

𝄽· = 𝄽 + 𝄾

▬· = ▬ + 𝄽

▬· = ▬ + ▬

A second dot adds a further quarter to the note or rest's original value.
When two dots are used, it is said to be **double-dotted**.

Notes

♪.. = ♪ + ♪ + ♪

♩.. = ♩ + ♪ + ♪

𝅗𝅥.. = 𝅗𝅥 + ♩ + ♪

𝅝.. = 𝅝 + 𝅗𝅥 + ♩

o·· = o + 𝅗𝅥 + ♩

Rests

𝄿·· = 𝄿 + 𝄿 + 𝄿

𝄾·· = 𝄾 + 𝄿 + 𝄿

𝄽·· = 𝄽 + 𝄾 + 𝄿

▬·· = ▬ + 𝄽 + 𝄾

▬·· = ▬ + ▬ + 𝄽

Tied notes

The duration of a note can also be increased by tying one note-value to
another of the same pitch. A tie ⌣ is a curved line that adds the values
of both notes together to make one sustained note. A tie is often used to
join notes that are sustained across a **bar-line** or **measure** (see 'Bars and
bar-lines' below).

𝅗𝅥 𝅗𝅥 = 𝅗𝅥 + 𝅗𝅥 = 𝅗𝅥.

♩ ♪ = ♩ + ♪ = ♩.

> There are rules governing when to use ties
> and when to use dotted notes (see pages
> 10, 11–12). Ties are never used on rests.

Bars and bar-lines

Music is divided up into **bars** (sometimes known as **measures**) that contain a specified number of **beats**. The bars are separated by **bar-lines**.

The word **pulse** is used to describe the underlying beat in a piece of music. When we beat time to a piece of music we are marking the main beats in a bar – the strongest accent is on the first beat. Music with:

- **two** beats in a bar is in **duple time**.
- **three** beats in a bar is in **triple time**.
- **four** beats in a bar is in **quadruple time**.

A beat may have the duration of a minim, crotchet, quaver, or any other note-value. The most common beat-value is the crotchet.

Introducing time signatures

The time signature is found at the beginning of a piece of music immediately *after* the key signature (see page 36). It tells you:

- the **number** of beats in each bar
- the **note-value** of the beat.

 The top number of a time signature shows the number of beats per bar.
The bottom number of a time signature shows the note-value of the beat: $2 = \downarrow$ *beat* $4 = \downarrow$ *beat* $8 = \eighthnote$ *beat*

Unlike the key signature, the time signature is not found at the beginning of every line of music. If the time signature stays the same throughout a piece, it is only written once. However, if the time of the music changes, a new time signature is needed.

> Time signatures have been used in Western music since about 1700.

Simple time signatures

Simple time signatures usually use a quaver, a crotchet, a minim, or another un-dotted note as the main beat. This means that the beats are divisible into halves, e.g.:

Depending on the number of main beats in a bar, simple time can be further grouped into **simple duple** (two beats), **simple triple** (three beats) and **simple quadruple** (four beats):

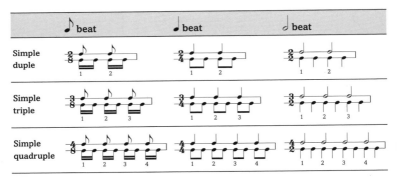

Notice the difference between the time signatures $\frac{2}{4}$ and the relatively rare $\frac{4}{8}$. Although they both use four quavers in a bar, $\frac{2}{4}$ has two crotchet beats per bar and $\frac{4}{8}$ has four quaver beats per bar.

> **'Four on the floor'** is a $\frac{4}{4}$ rhythm often used in disco and electronic dance music. It uses a bass drum on each beat of the bar.

Common time and split common time

$\frac{4}{4}$ (four crotchet beats in a bar) is the most common time signature and is also known as **common time**. This is sometimes shown by a letter **C**:

The sign **¢** indicates $\frac{2}{2}$ (two minim beats in a bar). It is often referred to as **split common time**.

> The word **'backbeat'** is used to describe the rhythmic emphasis on beats 2 and 4 within a four-beat bar. Many rock drum patterns are built around the kick (bass) drum sounding on beats 1 and 3 with the snare drum on the backbeat (beats 2 and 4).

Compound time signatures

Compound time signatures use a dotted note as the main beat; this is often a dotted crotchet. $\frac{6}{8}$, $\frac{9}{8}$ and $\frac{12}{8}$ are all compound time signatures with dotted crotchet beats. In compound time signatures, the dotted beat is divisible by three:

- When the main beat is a dotted crotchet, the quavers are grouped in threes (as above).
- When the main beat is a dotted minim, the crotchets are grouped in threes.
- When the main beat is a dotted quaver, the semiquavers are grouped in threes.

Depending on the number of main beats in a bar, compound time can be further categorised into **compound duple** (two dotted beats), **compound triple** (three dotted beats) and **compound quadruple** (four dotted beats):

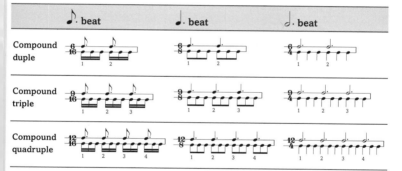

Notice the difference between the time signatures $\frac{3}{4}$ and $\frac{6}{8}$. Although they both use six quavers in a bar, $\frac{3}{4}$ has three crotchet beats per bar and $\frac{6}{8}$ has two dotted crotchet beats per bar. Here is the same passage using the same note-values, but written in $\frac{3}{4}$ and $\frac{6}{8}$:

Swung rhythm

Swung rhythms are found in jazz and blues as well as some types of pop music. In each pair of notes, the first is played a little longer than the second. Pairs of quavers in $\frac{4}{4}$, for instance, typically sound like a lazy $\frac{12}{8}$ when swung: although the music would be notated as:

it would be played as something closer to:

Plan B's song 'She Said' (2010) uses swung rhythms in the verse and straight rhythms in the rap chorus.

> The jazz trumpeter and singer Louis Armstrong was one of the first musicians to use $\frac{12}{8}$ swung rhythms. These can be heard in his early 1920s recordings with the King Oliver Band.

Time signatures with irregular divisions

All of the above time signatures have regular divisions into two, three or four beats per bar. Occasionally time signatures are used that have irregular divisions.

> Irregular metres are often found in folk music.

Quintuple time

In $\frac{5}{4}$ and $\frac{5}{8}$ the five beats are grouped into either 2 + 3 or 3 + 2.

- 'Take Five' (1959) by Paul Desmond is a well-known song in $\frac{5}{4}$ – some of the bars use a 2+3 metre and others use 3+2. Popularised by the Dave Brubeck Quartet, it quickly became a jazz standard.

- 'Hangin' Tree' (2002) by Queens of the Stone Age is in quintuple time and follows a 3+2 metre.

Septuple time

In $\frac{7}{4}$ and $\frac{7}{8}$ the seven beats can be grouped into various combinations of two, three and four, e.g. 2 + 3 + 2, or 3 + 2 + 2, or 4 + 3.

- Pink Floyd's song 'Money' (1973) has a time signature of $\frac{7}{4}$. The famous bass riff follows a 3+4 pattern.
- 'Ethiopia' (2011) by the band Red Hot Chili Peppers is predominantly in $\frac{7}{8}$. The opening bass riff follows a 4+3 pattern.

Grouping notes and rests

Notes and rests are grouped together in ways that make it easier to see where the beats are, so that the music is clearer to read. For example:

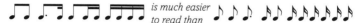

is much easier to read than

There are certain standard conventions that are usually followed when grouping notes and rests.

Grouping notes in simple time

Beams

In $\frac{2}{4}$, $\frac{3}{4}$ and $\frac{4}{4}$, notes belonging to the same crotchet beat should be beamed together so that the beats can be clearly picked out by the eye.

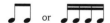

A crotchet beat made up of demisemiquavers can be grouped in either of two ways:

The beamed notes do not have to be of the same duration:

A beam should not normally extend beyond a beat because it becomes difficult to see where the beat divisions are:

Correct   Incorrect

However, it is acceptable to beam together complete bars of quavers in $\frac{2}{4}$ or $\frac{3}{4}$:

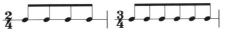

Complete bars of semiquavers in $\frac{3}{8}$ may also be beamed together:

In $\frac{4}{4}$ complete bars of quavers should be beamed into two groups of four. They should not be grouped together as this would make the music more difficult to read.

The same applies to bars in $\frac{4}{4}$ containing mixed note-values: beams should be avoided across the middle of the bar so that the two halves of the bar are clearly indicated:

> When grouping notes in $\frac{4}{4}$, it may help to think of an invisible line down the middle of the bar.

Ties

In simple time, ties between notes should be avoided where possible:

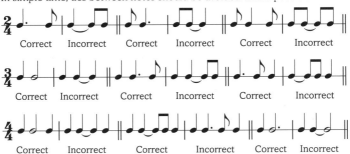

Grouping notes in compound time

Beams

In $\frac{6}{8}$, $\frac{9}{8}$ and $\frac{12}{8}$, notes shorter than a dotted crotchet should be beamed together so that the beats can be clearly picked out by the eye. Notes belonging to the same dotted crotchet beat are beamed together. Here are some common groupings of quavers, dotted quavers and semiquavers in compound time. All of them are grouped into dotted crotchet beats:

Quavers and shorter notes are beamed in such a way that the dotted-beat groupings are clear:

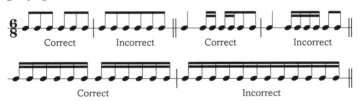

Correct Incorrect Correct Incorrect

Correct Incorrect

Ties

In compound time, ties are often necessary in order to notate the rhythmic duration of a note. The following passage would be impossible to write without using ties:

Ties between notes in compound time are also used to signpost where the main (dotted) beats are:

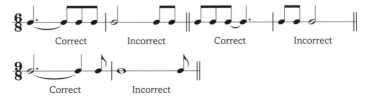

Correct Incorrect Correct Incorrect

Correct Incorrect

Notes lasting a whole bar are written as follows in $\frac{6}{8}$, $\frac{9}{8}$ and $\frac{12}{8}$:

Notice that a tie is required to notate a whole-bar note in $\frac{9}{8}$.

> Composers and songwriters do not always follow these rules, so you
> may be able to find unconventional groupings in music you are playing.

Grouping rests in simple time

In general, every main beat should have a rest of its own – rests of longer
than a beat should be avoided. Thus:

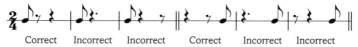

Correct   Incorrect   Incorrect   Correct   Incorrect   Incorrect

However, a clear half-bar at the beginning or end of a bar in $\frac{4}{4}$ can be
shown by a minim rest:

Correct   Correct   Correct   Incorrect

Grouping rests in compound time

In compound time, one rest may be used for the first and second divisions
of the beat together, but not for the second and third together:

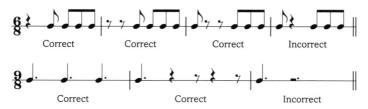

Correct   Correct   Correct   Incorrect

Correct   Correct   Incorrect

In $\frac{6}{8}$, $\frac{9}{8}$ and $\frac{12}{8}$, a silence lasting for a dotted crotchet beat may have a
rest of its own 𝄽 or be shown as 𝄽 𝄾, although the former is generally
considered clearer. Rests that are longer than a beat should be avoided:

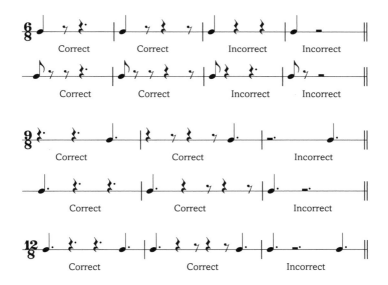

A clear half-bar at the beginning or end of a bar in $\frac{12}{8}$ can be shown by a dotted minim rest:

Whole-bar rests

A whole-bar rest is always shown by a semibreve rest, whatever the time signature:

Irregular note groupings

Irregular note groupings are sometimes found within a regular pulse. Commonly used irregular groupings are **duplets**, **triplets**, **quintuplets** and **sextuplets**.

Triplets and duplets

Beats are divisible into halves in simple time and into thirds in compound time. However, sometimes a composer/songwriter may wish to divide a beat up into thirds in simple time – i.e. so that three notes are played in the time of two. Such subdivisions are called triplets.

The triplet is indicated by the number **3** above or below the notes to which they apply. Triplet quavers and semiquavers are beamed together; triplet crotchets and minims are grouped with a bracket ⌐‾‾‾¬ or, less commonly today, a slur ⌒ above or below the notes.

Triplets are not always made up of notes of the same value. In the following example, bar 3 uses triplets made up of a crotchet and a quaver:

Other irregular note groupings

The other irregular note groups found most frequently are **quintuplets (5)**, **sextuplets (6)** and **septuplets (7)**. In every case, the irregular note group is played in the time of a simple-time note-value – i.e. a quaver, a crotchet or a minim.

In this extract, quintuplets, sextuplets and septuplets are written in semiquavers, as each of the groupings takes place over the time of a crotchet (or four-semiquaver) beat.

Quadruplets, where four notes are played in time of three, are usually found in compound time. They are shown by the figure **4** placed above or below the four notes:

(musical notation in 12/8 time)

> ### Irregular note-groupings: some guidelines
> - Triplets are written in values applicable to two of the same kind – 3:2.
> - Quintuplets, sextuplets and septuplets are written in values applicable to four of the same kind – 5:4, 6:4, 7:4.
> - 9, 10, 11, 13 and 15-note groups are written in values applicable to eight of the same kind – 9:8, 10:8, etc.

Syncopation

Syncopation is the effect created when off-beat notes are accented. It can be found in virtually every rock and pop song and may be produced in the following ways:

- **By placing a stress on a weak beat or between beats.** The following example of a classic rock rhythm contains a stress on the fourth quaver of the first bar:

This ragtime piece by Scott Joplin puts the stress in between beats 1 and 2 in the first full bar:

Extract from The Entertainer *(1902) by Scott Joplin*

- **By beginning a note on a weak beat and holding it over onto a strong beat.** In the following example, the final quaver of bar 1 is tied over onto the first (strong) beat of bar 2:

- **By putting a rest on a normally strong beat.** In the following example, the melody begins with a rest; this has the effect of displacing the beat of the music that follows:

Pitch

'What makes a tune tuneful? We have rhythm, but we need another ingredient. The answer is, of course, pitch. Pitch is the word we use to describe high and low sounds and it is the ingredient that turns rhythm into melody. Pitch is anything to do with the range of notes that combine to make those tunes sound tuneful. What makes a 'good' tune is an interesting question! Something to ponder on …'

Paul Harris

The stave

In music, the word **pitch** is used to describe how high or low a sound is. Each pitch is classified as a particular note that can be represented visually through music notation. Sounds of different pitches are represented as **notes** that are placed on a **stave** (or **staff**). The five-lined stave consists of five parallel lines with four equal spaces between them.

The five-lined stave

Higher pitch
⇕
Lower pitch

Notes are positioned on the lines or in the spaces: the higher up a note is positioned on the stave, the higher the pitch; the lower down, the lower the pitch.

Note names

Notes are named, in ascending order, by the first seven letters of the alphabet: A up to G. These letter names are then repeated to represent equivalent notes at a higher or lower level (or 'octave' – see page 24).

Lower pitch   *Higher pitch*

Piano keyboard showing note names

Treble clef

Clefs are written at the start of the stave and tell you what pitches (or notes), are being shown. When the **treble clef** sign (𝄞) is used, the note names are as follows:

> The treble clef is sometimes known as the G clef because the clef curls around the note G.

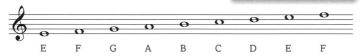

E   F   G   A   B   C   D   E   F

When the treble clef is used:

- the notes on the lines are E, G, B, D, F.

- the notes in the spaces are F, A, C, E.

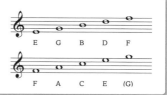

Bass clef

A different clef is used to write lower notes: 𝄢. This is known as the **bass clef**. When the bass clef is used, the note names are as follows:

> The bass clef is sometimes known as the F clef because the two dots are on either side of the note F.

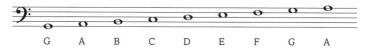

G   A   B   C   D   E   F   G   A

When the bass clef is used:

- the notes on the lines are G, B, D, F, A.

- the notes in the spaces are A, C, E, G.

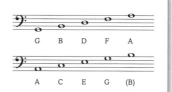

Middle C

The C nearest the centre of the piano keyboard is often referred to as **middle C**. It is also the pitch that falls exactly between the bottom of the treble clef and the top of the bass clef:

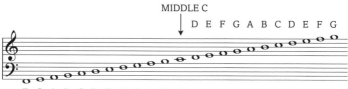

Ledger lines

Ledger lines are short lines above or below the stave; they are used whenever the note is too high or too low to be written on the stave. In the treble and bass clef, middle C is written with a ledger line.

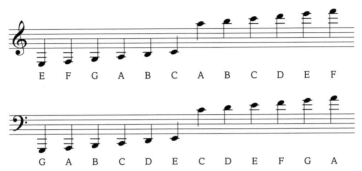

Notes with ledger lines in the treble and bass clefs

Stems

Many note symbols have a **stem**; how stems are positioned relates directly to where a note is positioned on the stave. When a note is pitched:

- above the middle line of the stave, the stem points downwards and joins to the left of the note head.

- below the middle line of the stave, the stem points upwards and joins to the right of the note head.

- on the middle line of the stave, the stem may point either upwards or downwards.

Alto and tenor clefs

The most commonly used clefs are the treble (G) clef and the bass (F) clef. Two other clefs that are in regular use today are the **alto clef** and the **tenor clef**. These are both C clefs because the line they are centred on is middle C.

Middle C written in the alto clef

The alto clef is used by the viola.

The tenor clef is used by cellos, double basses, bassoons and tenor trombones when they are playing in their upper register but they use the bass clef most of the time.

Middle C written in the tenor clef

Below is the same melody written at the same pitch in the four different clefs. It has been used in several films including the Beatles movie *Help!* (1965), *A Clockwork Orange* (1971) and the *Die Hard* franchise (1988 onwards).

Treble clef

Alto clef

Tenor clef

Bass clef

Extract from Beethoven's Ode to Joy *(Symphony No. 9)*

Accidentals: sharps, flats and naturals

Each note written on a stave can have its pitch slightly raised or lowered by the addition of an **accidental**.

A **sharp** (♯) placed before a note raises its pitch by one semitone (see page 34).

A **flat** (♭) lowers its pitch by one semitone.

A **natural** (♮) restores a note, previously sharpened or flattened, to its original pitch.

D sharp (raised)

D flat (lowered)

D natural (restored)

Notes that sound the same but are written (or 'spelt') differently are said to be **enharmonic**. For instance C♯ and D♭ are enharmonic equivalents.

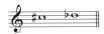

Theory in practice: using accidentals

Here are some guidelines for you to follow when you are reading or writing music:

- Accidentals are written before the note, even though we say them after (e.g. 'B flat').

- Accidentals remain in effect until the end of the bar, unless cancelled or overwritten by a subsequent sign.

- Accidentals *do not* apply to the same note at a different octave or in a different part.

- Accidentals on tied notes remain in effect until the end of the tied note, even where the note is sustained over a bar line.

- To restore a note to its original pitch, the accidental is cancelled by the appropriate natural, flat or sharp sign.

- Double flats and double sharps are cancelled in the same way. Note that only one natural sign is needed.

Double flats and double sharps

Sometimes it is necessary to sharpen a note that has already been sharpened, or to flatten a note that has already been flattened.

- A **double sharp** (×) placed before a note raises its pitch by two semitones.

G double sharp is the enharmonic equivalent of A

- A **double flat** (♭♭) lowers its pitch by two semitones.

A double flat is the enharmonic equivalent of G

> A double sharp is used in the G sharp minor scale, where the seventh (G♯), the leading note, is sharpened a further semitone to become G double sharp.

Intervals

An **interval** is the distance between two notes. If two notes are played together they form a **harmonic interval**; if they are played separately, they form a **melodic interval**.

harmonic   melodic
interval   interval

Intervals are measured by the total number of letter names found, starting with the lower note and going up to the higher note. Thus:

- C up to D is a **2nd**.
- C up to E (C D E) is a **3rd**.

> Both notes of the interval are included in the count.

Intervals in the major scale

All major scales (see page 35) are made from the same pattern of intervals. There are two kinds of intervals in the major scale: major intervals and perfect intervals.

Major intervals: 2nd (a tone), 3rd, 6th and 7th

Perfect intervals: 4th, 5th and octave.
Perfect intervals have a pure, rather hollow sound.

> There is no such thing as a major 4th or major 5th.

Here are the names of all of the intervals found between the tonic (key-note) of C major and the other degrees of the C major scale.

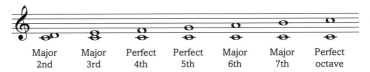

Major	Major	Perfect	Perfect	Major	Major	Perfect
2nd	3rd	4th	5th	6th	7th	octave

Other intervals

Either of the notes forming an interval may be sharpened or flattened to create a different kind of interval.

Minor intervals

Major intervals become **minor** when they are decreased by a semitone:

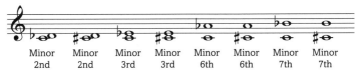

Minor	Minor	Minor	Minor	Minor	Minor	Minor	Minor
2nd	2nd	3rd	3rd	6th	6th	7th	7th

> A minor 2nd is the same interval as a semitone (see page 34).
> A minor 7th is sometimes known as the **subtonic**.

Diminished intervals

Perfect intervals become **diminished** when they are decreased by a semitone:

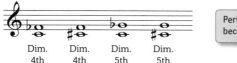

> Perfect intervals never become minor.

Minor 3rds and 7ths may be further flattened by a semitone and become **diminished**:

Augmented intervals

Major 2nds and 6ths and all perfect intervals become **augmented** when they are increased by a semitone:

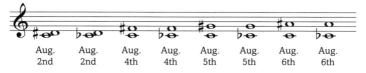

The tritone

The interval of the augmented 4th or diminished 5th is made up of three tones (C to D, D to E, E to F♯/G♭) and is therefore known as a **tritone**:

> The tritone is sometimes known as the *diabolus in musica* or 'the devil's interval' because of its dissonant, unstable quality. Jimi Hendrix uses it in 'Purple Haze' (1967).

Theory in practice: naming and writing intervals

The intervals found between the tonic (key-note) of a major key and
the other degrees of the scale serve as a useful standard by which other
intervals can be worked out.

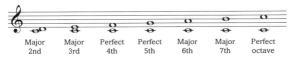

| Major | Major | Perfect | Perfect | Major | Major | Perfect |
| 2nd | 3rd | 4th | 5th | 6th | 7th | octave |

Always name the interval from the lower note. Think of the lower note as
though it is the tonic or key-note.

Example 1: G to D

1   2   3   4   5   6   7   8

To name this interval, think of G as the tonic of a G major scale. D is the
fifth degree of the G major scale, making this interval a **perfect 5th**.

Example 2: D to C

1   2   3   4   5   6   7   8

To name this interval, think of D as the tonic of a D major scale. C♯ is the
seventh degree of the D major scale (a major 7th). C is a semitone lower
than C♯, so this interval is a **minor 7th**.

Example 3: C♯ to E

1   2   3   4   5   6   7   8

To name this interval, if you do not know the key signature of C♯ major,
think instead of the C major scale. E is the third degree of the C major
scale – a major 3rd above C. C♯ is a semitone higher than C, so the
interval is a **minor 3rd**.

Table of intervals

Compound intervals

All of the intervals mentioned so far have been of an octave or less and are sometimes called **simple intervals**. Intervals that are wider than an octave are known as **compound intervals**.

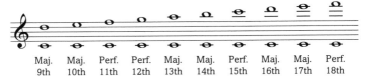

| Maj. | Maj. | Perf. | Perf. | Maj. | Maj. | Perf. | Maj. | Maj. | Perf. |
| 9th | 10th | 11th | 12th | 13th | 14th | 15th | 16th | 17th | 18th |

Compound intervals

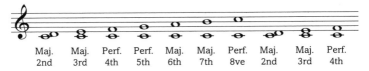

| Maj. | Maj. | Perf. | Perf. | Maj. | Maj. | Perf. | Maj. | Maj. | Perf. |
| 2nd | 3rd | 4th | 5th | 6th | 7th | 8ve | 2nd | 3rd | 4th |

Corresponding simple intervals

Compound intervals keep the same qualities as the corresponding simple intervals. So a 9th from C to D is a major 9th, an 11th from C to F is a perfect 11th, and so on.

Naming compound intervals

Compound intervals can be numbered in two ways:

1 By including the octave as in the first example above: major 9th, major 10th, perfect 11th, and so on

2 By subtracting the octave(s) as in the second example above: compound major 2nd, compound major 3rd, compound perfect 4th, and so on

> To calculate the number of a compound interval, subtract 7 from the larger number. For example, a perfect 12th is a compound perfect 5th (12 minus 7).

Enharmonic intervals

Some notes sound the same as each other but are written (or 'spelt')
differently; these are said to be '**enharmonic**'. For example, the augmented
4th and the diminished 5th are enharmonic equivalents because the F♯
sounds the same as the G♭.

Aug. 4th   Dim. 5th

Consonant and dissonant intervals

Harmonic intervals can be classified as **consonant** or **dissonant**.

Dissonant intervals feel somewhat unstable, as though one of the notes
needs to move up or down to resolve into a consonance. The major 7th,
for example, feels as though it needs to resolve upwards, and the minor
7th feels as though it needs to resolve downwards.

Major 7th   Minor 7th

Major and minor 2nds, perfect 4ths, major and minor 7ths and all
augmented and diminished intervals are **dissonant**.

Consonant intervals feel relatively stable and do not need to resolve to
another interval. Major and minor 3rds and 6ths, perfect 5ths and octaves
are all consonant intervals. Two voices producing exactly the same pitch
are said to be in **unison**.

Table of intervals and music examples

Interval	Ascending/ descending	Music example
Minor 2nd	ascending	'A Hard Day's Night' by the Beatles
		'Jaws' film theme by John Williams
Minor 2nd	descending	'Joy To The World' (Christmas song)
Major 2nd	ascending	'Happy Birthday' by Mildred and Patty Hill
Major 2nd	descending	'Yesterday' by the Beatles
Minor 3rd	ascending	'Greensleeves' (trad.)
Minor 3rd	descending	'Hey Jude' by the Beatles
Major 3rd	ascending	'Morning Has Broken' (trad.)
Major 3rd	descending	'Summertime' by George Gershwin
Perfect 4th	ascending	'Amazing Grace' (trad.)
Perfect 4th	descending	'O Come All Ye Faithful' (Christmas carol)
Tritone	ascending	'The Simpsons' theme tune by Danny Elfman
		'Maria' from *West Side Story* by Leonard Bernstein
Tritone	descending	'Close Every Door To Me' from *Joseph* by Andrew Lloyd Webber (notes 4–5)

(continued)

Interval	Ascending/ descending	Music example
Perfect 5th	ascending	*2001: A Space Odyssey* film theme by Richard Strauss
Perfect 5th	descending	'What Shall We Do With The Drunken Sailor?' on the word 'drunk-en' (trad.)
Minor 6th	ascending	'The Entertainer' by Scott Joplin (notes 3–4)
Minor 6th	descending	*Love Story* film theme by Francis Lai
Major 6th	ascending	'My Way' (Frank Sinatra)
Major 6th	descending	'Nobody Knows The Trouble I've Seen' (African-American spirtual)
Minor 7th	ascending	'Somewhere' from *West Side Story* by Leonard Bernstein
Minor 7th	descending	'An American in Paris' by George Gershwin
Major 7th	ascending	'Somewhere Over The Rainbow' by Harold Arlen (notes 1 and 3)
Major 7th	descending	'I Love You' by Cole Porter (notes 2 and 3)
Octave	ascending	'Somewhere Over The Rainbow' by Harold Arlen (notes 1 and 2)
Octave	descending	'There's No Business Like Show Business' by Irving Berlin (notes 2 and 3)

Theory in practice: recognising intervals – listening

Harmonic intervals

You can learn to recognise harmonic intervals by:

- listening to the two notes and separating them
- listening for consonances and dissonances.

Melodic intervals

When identifying a melodic interval, you may find it helpful to:

- sing up a scale in your head, starting on the note of the lower interval, until you reach the upper note
- think of a melody that opens with that interval.

Scales

'Scales, and all their musical relations (arpeggios, broken chords and so on), are patterns of related pitches that we use to create melody. They come in many different guises, each of which creates its own unique sound-world. Call any song you like to mind, and you'll almost certainly find that it uses scale patterns.

Paul Harris

Introducing scales

A **scale** is a pattern of notes arranged in order, from low to high (or vice versa).

Major and **minor** scales are known as **diatonic** scales and are built on patterns of seven notes within an octave span (see page 24). These patterns, which are built on a combination of **tones** and **semitones** (see below), give each kind of scale a characteristic sound.

The degrees of the scale

First degree	**Tonic**	Key-note
Second degree	**Supertonic**	The note above the tonic
Third degree	**Mediant**	The note midway between the tonic and the dominant
Fourth degree	**Subdominant**	The note below the dominant
Fifth degree	**Dominant**	Next in importance to the tonic
Sixth degree	**Submediant**	The note above the dominant
Seventh degree	**Leading note**	The note leading to the tonic

Tones and semitones

Tones and semitones are measurements of pitch. There are semitones between all adjacent notes on a keyboard, whether black or white. A tone consists of two semitones.

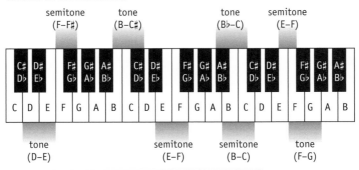

There are two places in each octave where there is a semitone between two neighbouring white notes: B–C and E–F.

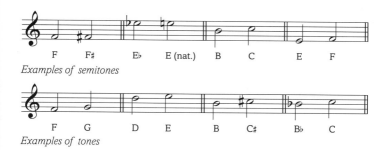

F   F♯   E♭   E (nat.)   B   C   E   F

Examples of semitones

F   G   D   E   B   C♯   B♭   C

Examples of tones

Major scales

All major scales are built on the following pattern:

tone   tone   semitone   tone   tone   tone   semitone

The semitones come between the 3rd and 4th degrees of the scale and between the 7th degree and the octave.

Here is the scale of C major – it uses only the white notes on the keyboard:

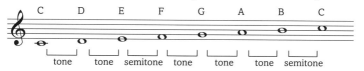

C   D   E   F   G   A   B   C

tone   tone   semitone   tone   tone   tone   semitone

> The major scale uses the same pattern of notes as the Ionian mode (see page 145 for the Table of Modes).

The major scale can be reproduced at any pitch, meaning that it can start on any note. Here is the scale of G major:

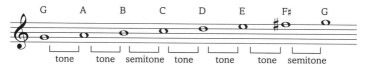

G   A   B   C   D   E   F♯   G

tone   tone   semitone   tone   tone   tone   semitone

Notice that an F♯ is needed in order to keep to the correct pattern of tones and semitones, i.e. so that there is a semitone between the leading note (F♯) and the tonic (G).

Here is the scale of F major:

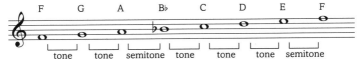

Notice that a B♭ is needed in order to keep to the correct pattern of tones and semitones.

Key signatures

When a piece of music is based on a particular scale, it is said to be in the key of that scale. For example, a work in the key of G major will use the notes found in the G major scale, meaning that F♯s rather than F♮s will be used throughout, unless otherwise indicated. Instead of writing a ♯ sign every time an F♯ is used, this is shown as a **key signature**:

Key signature for G major

The same principle applies to music in any key.

A key signature is positioned:
- at the beginning of *every* line of music.
- *after* the clef.
- *before* the time signature.

> Ledger lines are *never* used in a key signature.

Key signatures of the sharp major keys

Notice that:
- the sharps always appear in the same order: F♯ C♯ G♯ D♯ A♯ E♯ (count *up* a 5th from the preceding one).
- the final sharp is the leading note of the key. For instance, the final sharp of E major is D♯.
- each new key is a 5th above the preceding one. For instance, A major has three sharps and E major (a 5th above) has four sharps.

Key signatures of the flat major keys

C   F   B♭   E♭   A♭   D♭   G♭   C♭

Notice that:

- the flats always appear in the same order: B♭ E♭ A♭ D♭ G♭ C♭ (count *down* a 5th from the preceding one).
- the penultimate flat is on the same note as the key. For instance, the penultimate flat of A♭ major is on A.
- each new key is a 5th below the preceding one. For instance, A♭ major has four flats and E♭ major (a 5th below) has three flats.

Major scales notated without key signatures - sharp keys

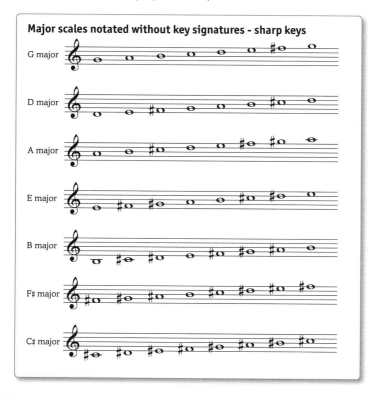

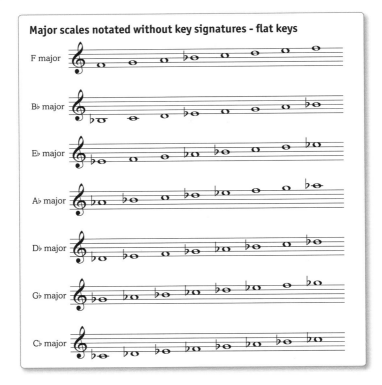

Major scales notated without key signatures - flat keys

F major

B♭ major

E♭ major

A♭ major

D♭ major

G♭ major

C♭ major

Minor scales

There are three different versions of each minor key:

- the **natural** minor
- the **harmonic** minor
- the **melodic** minor

Each type of minor scale follows a different pattern of intervals, but always includes a minor 3rd between the tonic and the mediant (the first and third degrees of the scale). This minor 3rd helps to give the minor keys their characteristic sound.

Natural minor

All natural minor scales are built on the following pattern. The notes are the same, whether ascending or descending.

tone   semitone   tone   tone   semitone   tone   tone

The semitones come between the 2nd and 3rd, and the 5th and 6th degrees of the scale. This is the same sequence of tones and semitones given by the white notes of the piano, from A to A.

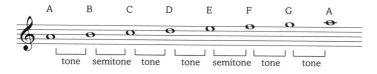

> The natural minor is found most often in pop music, folk and jazz. It uses the same pattern of notes as the Aeolian mode (see page 145 of the Table of Modes).

Here is the scale of C natural minor:

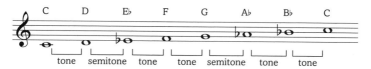

Notice that ♭s are needed on E, A and B in order to keep to the correct pattern of tones and semitones.

Harmonic minor

Harmonic minor scales are built on the following pattern. The notes are the same, whether ascending or descending.

tone   semitone   tone   tone   semitone   tone and a half   semitone

The semitones come between the 2nd and 3rd degrees of the scale and the 7th and octave. There is a tone and a half between the 6th and 7th degrees of the scale.

Here is the scale of A harmonic minor:

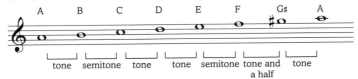

> The harmonic minor scale is so-called because it can be used to harmonise the three primary triads I, IV and V (see page 52).

Melodic minor

Melodic minor scales are built on the following pattern. Unlike the major, natural and harmonic minor scales, the pattern is different when ascending and descending.

Ascending:
tone   semitone   tone   tone   tone   tone   semitone

The semitones come between the 2nd and 3rd degrees of the scale and the 7th and octave.

Descending:
tone   tone   semitone   tone   tone   semitone   tone

The semitones come between the 2nd and 3rd degrees of the scale and the 5th and 6th.

Here is the scale of A melodic minor, ascending and descending.

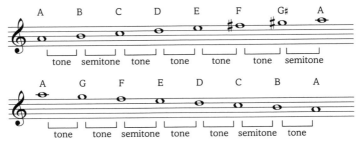

> The melodic minor does not include the leap of a tone and a half (augmented 2nd) – this enables a smoother melody line.

Relative major and minor keys

Major and minor keys with the same key signatures are said to be **related**. So:

- C major is the **relative major** of A minor.
- A minor is the **relative minor** of C major.

The key signature of a minor key is found by going up a tone and a half (a **minor 3rd**) from the tonic – this is the key-note of the relative major. So:

- The key signature of C minor is the same as the key signature of Eb major.
- The key signature of D minor is the same as the key signature of F major.

Sharp keys			Flat keys		
C major	A minor	𝄞	C major	A minor	𝄞
G major	E minor	𝄞	F major	D minor	𝄞
D major	B minor	𝄞	Bb major	G minor	𝄞
A major	F♯ minor	𝄞	Eb major	C minor	𝄞
E major	C♯ minor	𝄞	Ab major	F minor	𝄞
B Major	G♯ minor	𝄞	Db major	Bb minor	𝄞
F♯ major	D♯ minor	𝄞	Gb major	Eb minor	𝄞
C♯ major	A♯ minor	𝄞	Cb major	Ab minor	𝄞

Table of key signatures – major and minor

Tonic major and tonic minor

When a major and minor key both have the same key-note (tonic), one is said to be the **tonic major** or **tonic minor** of the other. So:

- C major is the **tonic major** of C minor.
- D minor is the **tonic minor** of D major.

The circle of fifths

The circle of fifths is a useful way of demonstrating the relationship between different keys.

- The **primary triads** (I, IV and V – see page 52) of any key can be found by looking on either side of the key-note (tonic). For instance, in the key of C, the two adjacent keys are G (**V** – the **dominant**) and F (**IV** – the **subdominant**).
- The three most closely related keys are the **dominant** (V), the **sub-dominant** (IV) and the **relative minor or major**. When a piece of music changes key (or **modulates**), it is most likely to move to one of these keys.
- Three of the major keys (B, F♯, and D♭) have two spellings each – B/C♭, D♭/C♯ and F♯/G♭. These are called **enharmonic notes** (see page 29). The equivalent minor keys can also be spelt in two ways.

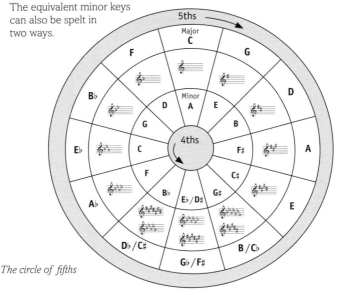

The circle of fifths

Theory in practice: identifying keys without a key signature

- Note down the accidentals used in the melody and write them in the order that they would appear in a key signature.
- Identify the key signature.
- Look at the melody again and decide whether it is in a major or minor key. If it is a minor key, you will probably find accidentals outside of the key signature, such as a sharpened leading note. The melody may also start or end on the key-note.

Chromatic scale

The chromatic scale is made up of all the twelve notes in an octave and is formed entirely of semitones. It may begin on any note. There are several different ways of writing a chromatic scale, but you should always include the following:

- at least one and not more than two notes on each line and space
- the unaltered subdominant (IV) and dominant (V)
- the sharpened subdominant (IV).

There are various ways to write a chromatic scale. The most common form is written as follows:

Ascending

This is sometimes known as the **harmonic chromatic scale**. Each letter name appears twice, apart from the tonic and dominant.

Descending

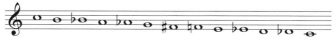

There are other ways of notating a chromatic scale – composers and song-writers usually write whatever is most convenient.

The word 'chromatic' comes from 'chroma', the Greek word for *colour*. A chromatic scale is so named because it is formed from a diatonic scale with added chromatic notes adding colour.

Pentatonic scales

Pentatonic scales have five notes. The word 'pentatonic' comes from the Greek word 'pente', meaning five. They are very common in folk music from around the world and are a useful basis for improvising in jazz, pop, and rock music as they work well over several chords.

Pentatonic major

The pentatonic major uses the same notes as a major scale, but omits the 4th and 7th degrees:

Pentatonic scale on C

> Pentatonic scales are also useful when improvising because they work well over several chords.

The notes of the pentatonic major scale correspond with the black notes of the keyboard starting on G♭:

Pentatonic scale on G♭

> Several song melodies by The Smiths are based on the pentatonic scale, including 'Heaven Knows I'm Miserable Now' (1984) and 'There Is A Light That Never Goes Out' (1986).

Riffs are frequently based on three or four notes drawn from the pentatonic scale. Here are some characteristic examples:

Pentatonic minor

The pentatonic minor uses the same notes as the natural minor scale, but omits the 2nd and 6th degrees:

Pentatonic minor scale on A

Pentatonic minor scale on C

The notes of the pentatonic minor scale correspond with the black notes of the keyboard starting on E♭:

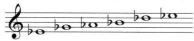

Pentatonic minor scale on E♭

Modes

Modes are seven-note scales. Each mode can be found by playing an octave of 'white notes' on the piano but with a different starting note, e.g. **D** E F G A B C, **G** A B C D E F, etc. Each mode follows a different pattern of tones and semitones.

> Major and natural minor scales are modes (the Ionian and Aeolian modes respectively) but the term is usually reserved for other seven-note scales.

Two of the most commonly used modes are the **Dorian** mode and the **Mixolydian** mode:

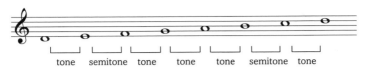

The Dorian mode

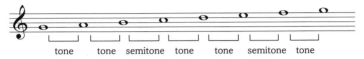

The Mixolydian mode

The D Mixolydian mode is used in 'Royals' (2013) by Lorde.

Modes can be transposed to start on any note. Here are the Dorian and Mixolydian modes starting on C:

Dorian mode starting on C

Mixolydian mode starting on C

A table of modes is provided in Appendix 1 (page 141).

The blues scale

The blues scale is not so much defined by the specific series of notes as by the use of certain notes characteristic of blues music (known as 'blue notes'). In the blues, notes from the major scale are flattened – commonly the 3rd, 5th and 7th – and this results in a six-note scale. Here is the blues scale in C (see Appendix 1, page 146 for other blues scales):

Blues scales in C

Blues songs may use both the flattened 3rd and the major 3rd for various parts of the music; for instance, the flattened 3rd may be used in the melody while at the same time the major 3rd is present in the backing. This results in an ambiguity between the major and minor so that the song is not to be felt in either. Likewise, the flattened 5th is used in addition to the fifth note of the major scale.

Whole-tone scale

The whole-tone scale is made up of six whole tones starting on either C or D♭ (its only transposition).

Whole-tone scale on C

Whole-tone scale on D♭

> Stevie Wonder uses a whole-tone scale in the intro to 'You Are The Sunshine Of My Life' (1972).

Octatonic scale

The octatonic scale is made up of eight notes alternating between tones and semitones:

Radiohead uses an octatonic scale in the intro to their song 'Just' (1995).

Chords and chord progressions

'Whenever two or more pitches sound at the same time, a chord is produced. Sometimes chords sound harmonious, agreeable or 'consonant'; at other times they might be tense, uncertain or 'dissonant'. So much of the emotional power of music is caused by the tensions and resolutions that are created by the progression between different consonant and dissonant chords.'

Paul Harris

Introducing chords and triads

The study of harmony centres on chords and their relationships to each other. A **chord** is the simultaneous sounding of two or more notes to produce harmony. Harmony is a fundamental element of Western music. The basic building block of harmony is the **triad**, a chord made up of three notes. The chord of C, for example, is made up of the notes C, E and G. C is the **root**, E is the **3rd**, because it is the third degree of the scale (counting up from the root) and G is the **5th**.

Tonic triads

The tonic triad is built on the tonic (or key-note) of a key. Here are the tonic triads of C, F and G major. They are all major chords:

Here are the tonic triads of A, D and E minor. They are all minor chords:

A triad can be formed on any degree of the scale (see page 34) and takes its name from that degree, e.g. dominant chord, tonic chord, and so on.

Major and minor triads

These are the two main kinds of triad. The major triad has a major 3rd from the root and the minor triad has a minor 3rd from the root. Both have perfect 5ths from the root.

major triad	=	**root**	+	**major 3rd**	+	**perfect 5th**
C major triad	=	*C*	+	*E*	+	*G*

minor triad	=	**root**	+	**minor 3rd**	+	**perfect 5th**
C minor triad	=	*C*	+	*E♭*	+	*G*

Power chords

Power chords are commonly found in rock music, often with distortion effects. 'You Really Got Me' (1964) by the Kinks is an example of a rock song built around power chords. Made up of just two pitches – the root and the 5th – power chords sound neither major nor minor due to the absence of a 3rd.

The root of a power chord is often doubled an octave higher:

E^5

> In folk music, the same chord is more often called the 'open fifth'.

Naming chords

In pop music, the chords of a song are indicated by letter names:

- A major chord is shown by writing the letter of the chord's root. For instance, C major is written as **C**.

- A minor chord uses the letter name of the root followed by a small 'm'. For instance, A minor is written as **Am**.

- Further information is added when needed to indicate harmonies other than the basic triads. For instance, a C major chord with the addition of the 6th above the root is written as **C6**.

> ### Roman numerals
>
> Roman numerals taken from the degrees of a scale are sometimes used to denote chords:
>
> | | | |
> |---|---|---|
> | Tonic | I | (e.g. C in the key of C major) |
> | Subdominant | IV | (e.g. F in the key of C major) |
> | Dominant | V | (e.g. G in the key of C major) |
>
> Although not often used in pop notation, they have the advantage of applying to a sequence of chords irrespective of the key. This means that you can play a chord progression from Roman numerals in any key. In the text below, both systems will be used.

Primary and secondary triads

The triads built upon the tonic, subdominant and dominant degrees are known as the **primary triads**. The primary triads are the most frequently used chords in Western music and help to establish the key most strongly.

> Chords built on the other degrees of the scale (II, III, VI and VII) are known as secondary **triads.**

Below are the primary triads of C major. Each chord has a major 3rd and a perfect 5th from the root and is therefore a **major chord**:

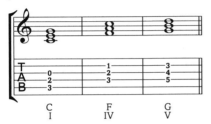

C
I

F
IV

G
V

> Roman numerals taken from the degrees of a scale are sometimes used to denote chords.

Chords I and IV in a minor key have a minor 3rd and a perfect 5th from the root and are therefore **minor** chords. However, chord V in a minor key has a major 3rd and a perfect 5th from the root and is therefore a **major** chord. Here are the primary triads of A minor:

Am
I

Dm
IV

E
V

> Notice the accidental on the 3rd in chord V (G#). This is used because it is the leading note in the harmonic minor scale (see page 39).

Many popular songs are built on the three primary triads, or the **three-chord trick**. The 12-bar blues (see page 64) is one of the most prevalent types of three-chord song.

> Status Quo is well known for their three-chord songs including 'Rockin' All Over The World' (1977).

Chord inversions and slash chords

When a chord is arranged with the root as the bass note, it is said to be in **root position**. This is commonly the case in pop music, especially in guitar-driven songs such as 'Seven Nation Army' (2003) by The White Stripes. However, chords can be arranged with notes other than the root at the bass; these chords are said to be in **inversion** and are shown by adding the bass-note name after the chord name.

- When the 3rd of the chord is the bass note, it is said to be in **first inversion**. The C major chord in first inversion is shown as **C/E**.

- When the 5th of the chord is the bass note, it is said to be in **second inversion**. The A minor chord in second inversion is shown as **Am/E**.

Roman numerals and chord inversions

Chord inversions can be shown by Roman numerals as follows:

- A first-inversion chord is shown by the letter 'b' after the Roman numeral, e.g. **Vb.**

- A second-inversion chord is shown by the letter 'c' after the Roman numeral, e.g. **Ic.**

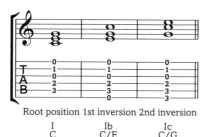

Root position   1st inversion   2nd inversion
    I   Ib   Ic
    C   C/E   C/G

The C major chord in root position, first inversion and second inversion

---

In pop music, chords in inversion are commonly referred to as **slash chords**. A slash chord is a sustained or repeated note that is sounded against changing harmonies: the bass note stays the same while the chords above it change. This is sometimes known as 'playing away from the chord' and can produce some complex harmonies.

> Slash chords are often used where the bass line is built on an ascending or descending scale. For instance 'A Whiter Shade Of Pale' (1967) by Procol Harum opens with a descending bass line: **C   C/B   Am   Am/G   F   F/E   D**

The chord notation usually identifies the bass note and the chord separately. The following chord progression uses a **tonic pedal**:

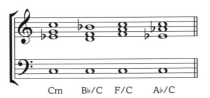

Cm   Bb/C   F/C   Ab/C

Major, minor, diminished and augmented chords

Triads are most frequently identified as one of four chord types: major, minor, diminished and augmented. They are made up of the following intervals:

major root = root + major 3rd + perfect 5th
minor root = root + minor 3rd + perfect 5th
diminished = root + minor 3rd + diminished 5th
augmented = root + major 3rd + augmented 5th

Here is an example of each type of chord built on C:

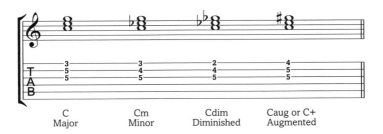

| C | Cm | Cdim | Caug or C+ |
| Major | Minor | Diminished | Augmented |

You could also think of a triad as being built up by putting two 3rds on top of each other. The two types of 3rds (major and minor) can be combined in four different ways:

1 A minor 3rd placed over a major 3rd produces a major chord.

2 A major 3rd over a minor 3rd produces a minor chord.

3 A minor 3rd over a minor 3rd produces a diminished chord.

4 A major 3rd over a major 3rd produces an augmented chord.

When triads are built on each degree of the **major scale**, the following types of chord result:

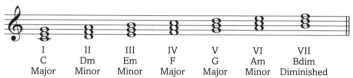

I	II	III	IV	V	VI	VII
C	Dm	Em	F	G	Am	Bdim
Major	Minor	Minor	Major	Major	Minor	Diminished

When triads are built on each degree of the **minor scale**, the following types of chord result:

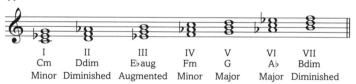

I	II	III	IV	V	VI	VII
Cm	Ddim	E♭aug	Fm	G	A♭	Bdim
Minor	Diminished	Augmented	Minor	Major	Major	Diminished

Seventh chords

Seventh chords are made by adding a 7th above the root on top of a triad. These are the seventh chords built on the different degrees of a C major scale (the 7th notes are shown in brackets on the guitar tab):

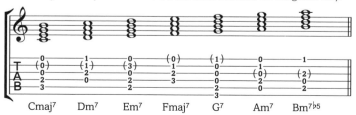

These are the seventh chords built on the different degrees of a C minor scale (the 7th notes are shown in brackets on the guitar tab):

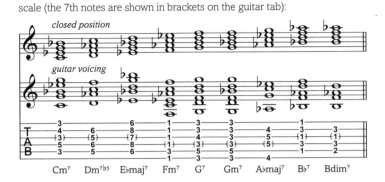

| Cm⁷ | Dm⁷ᵇ⁵ | E♭maj⁷ | Fm⁷ | G⁷ | Gm⁷ | A♭maj⁷ | B♭⁷ | Bdim⁷ |

There are five main types of seventh chord: the **dominant 7th**, the **major 7th**, the **minor 7th**, the **minor 7th flat 5** (or **half-diminished 7th**) and the **diminished 7th**.

1 The **seventh** is a major triad plus a minor 7th. When it is built on the fifth degree of the scale (the dominant) it is known as a **dominant seventh**.

2 The **major seventh** chord is a major triad plus a major 7th.

3 The **minor seventh** chord is minor triad plus a minor 7th.

4 The **minor seventh flat 5** (or half diminished seventh) is a diminished chord plus a minor 7th.

5 The **diminished seventh** chord is a diminished triad plus a diminished 7th.

Sus chords

In **suspended chords** (or **sus chords**) the 3rd of a major or minor chord is replaced by the 2nd or the 4th. The sound is neither major nor minor and sounds unresolved.

> In the verse of 'Pinball Wizard' (1969) by The Who, a series of sus chords is used:
> **Bsus4   B   Asus4   A   Gsus4   G   F#sus4   F#**

In Csus4 the 3rd of the chord (E)
is replaced by the 4th (F):

C^{sus4}

In Csus2, the 3rd of the chord (E)
is replaced by the 2nd (D):

C^{sus2}

Sus chords can also be built
on seventh chords:

G^{7sus4}

> The word 'sus' is short for 'suspension'. It comes from Classical harmony where suspensions have to resolve following a set of rules – such rules are often not applied in pop music.

More advanced chords

Extended chords

Extended chords add further notes to seventh chords.

Ninth, **eleventh** and **thirteenth** chords can be made by adding more thirds above the seventh chord:

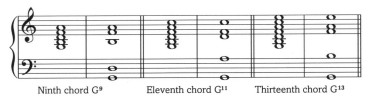

Ninth chord G^9 Eleventh chord G^{11} Thirteenth chord G^{13}

It is not necessary to play every note of these chords, and there are no rules to determine which notes should or shouldn't be omitted. However, it is usually advisable to include:
- the root
- the 3rd and/or 5th
- the 7th
- the note by which the chord is numbered (9th, 11th or 13th).

In the above example, the 3rd is omitted from the eleventh chord and the 5th and 11th are omitted from the thirteenth chord. The most commonly omitted note is the 5th.

Added chords

These are chords that contain extra notes that aren't part of the basic chord. The most common added chord (or add chord) is the **added 6th**, where a 6th is added to a major triad:

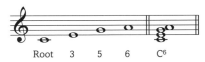

Root   3   5   6 C^6

The C6 chord

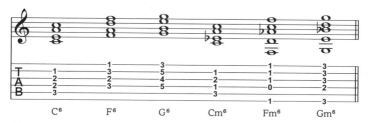

Major and minor chords with added 6ths

Substitution chords

Substitution chords are a device found most frequently in jazz. The term refers to chords that are interchangeable – where one chord can be substituted for a similar chord within a chord progression.

In the following example:
- the F chord has been substituted for Dm7 (D F A C), with which it has three notes in common (F A C).
- the second C chord has been substituted for Am7 (A C E G), with which it has three notes in common (C E G).

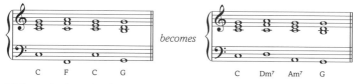

Major and minor chords with the same root have two notes in common and can be used as substitutions for each other, e.g. C (C E G) and Cm (C E♭ G).

Introducing cadences

Cadences are used to punctuate music, either bringing a melody to a point of repose before going on, or bringing it to a close. They are found at the end of musical phrases (see page 85) and serve a similar purpose to commas and full stops in a sentence. They are usually harmonised by two chords. The four main kinds of cadences are:

The **perfect cadence**	V–I
The **imperfect cadence**	Any chord followed by V (usually I–V, II–V or IV–V)
The **plagal cadence**	IV–I
The **interrupted cadence**	V followed by any chord (usually V–VI)

There are two cadences that end on the tonic chord: the perfect cadence and the plagal cadence. These cadences have the greatest sense of finality or completion.

The perfect cadence (V–I)

The perfect cadence (V–I) is frequently found at the end of pieces or sections of music. An example is the first movement of Beethoven's Symphony No. 5, which ends with eight perfect cadences played in succession. Another name for the perfect cadence is the **full close**.

V   I

A perfect cadence in C major

> The perfect cadence sometimes uses a dominant seventh (V7–I).

The sense of finality in a perfect cadence comes from two things:

1 The move from the dominant (e.g. G) to the tonic or 'key-note' (e.g. C)
2 The leading note (e.g. B) rising to the tonic (e.g. C)

The imperfect cadence (I–V, II–V or IV–V)

The imperfect cadence always ends on the dominant chord. The dominant can be preceded by any other chord to create an imperfect cadence, but the most common progressions are I–V, II–V and IV–V. Imperfect cadences sound unfinished and give the impression that the music is going to continue. Another name for the imperfect cadence is the **half close**.

An imperfect cadence in C major

The plagal cadence (IV–I)

The plagal cadence consists of the subdominant chord followed by the tonic chord. Similar to the perfect cadence, it gives a sense of completion.

A plagal cadence in C major

> Because the plagal cadence is often heard at the end of hymns on the word 'Amen', it is sometimes known as the 'Amen cadence'.

The interrupted cadence (V–?)

The use of the dominant chord in an interrupted cadence leads the listener to expect a perfect cadence; however, instead of being followed by the expected tonic chord, another chord (often the submediant) is used. For this reason, the interrupted cadence is sometimes known as a **false close** or **surprise cadence**.

An interrupted cadence

The cadential $^6_4$–$^5_3$ chord progression

The cadential $^6_4$–$^5_3$ chord progression is often used to approach a perfect or an imperfect cadence:

Cadence	Chords	Key of C	Key of G	Key of Em
Perfect	V–I	G–C	D–G	B–Em
Imperfect	I–V	C–G	G–D	Em–B
	II–V	Dm–G	Am–D	F#dim–B
	IV–V	F–G	C–D	Am–B
Plagal	IV–I	F–C	C–G	Am–Em
Interrupted	V–VI	G–Am	D–Em	B–C

Table of common cadences in three keys

Chord progressions

All music relies on a balance between repetition and contrast, something that is reflected in the harmonic structure of most popular songs.
Pop music often uses repeated sequences of chords known as chord progressions that tend to occur in cycles of two, four or eight bars. The 12-bar blues (see page 64) is an example of a song form that is structured around a repeated chord progression.

- Some of the strongest chord progressions move between chords whose roots are a 4th or 5th apart, or that descend by a 3rd.
- Stepwise chord progressions are often found in pop music, e.g. I–II–III–IV, which is C Dm Em F in the key of C.

- Sometimes chord progressions are built upon a pentatonic root-note sequence, e.g. A C D F G (see page 44).

> The rate at which chords change is known as **harmonic rhythm**. Chords usually change less often than the notes of the melody: a slower rate of chord-change can lead to a feeling of stasis and stability, whereas quick-changing chords can give a sense of speed and movement.

Verse and chorus

The verse-and-chorus song form is extremely common and uses harmony to help define its structure.

- The verse and chorus are usually based on different chord progressions.
- The chord progression for the **middle eight** (or **bridge**) generally ends on a dominant chord in order to lead into the next section.
- When a **turnaround** is used, it is often a short chord progression in its own right, with the crucial chord being the dominant.

> A **turnaround** is the final part of a section, in which the melody or chords prepare for the next section.

> A **middle eight** is a contrasting section in the middle of a song (not necessarily eight bars long) often with a different arrangement of instruments and in a different key.

One-chord songs

Some pop music is based around just one chord. Examples include Aretha Franklin's 'Chain Of Fools' (1968) and 'Tomorrow Never Knows' (1966) by the Beatles. Bob Marley's songs 'Exodus' (1977) and 'Get Up, Stand Up' (1973) are both based on the A minor chord.

Two-chord songs

Two-chord songs are common in reggae, where the musical interest tends to lie more in the rhythm than the harmony. Bob Marley's 'Lively Up Yourself' (1974), for instance, is based on the D7 and G7 chords. There are also many pop songs where either the verse or chorus is built on two chords, such as Michael Jackson's 'Beat It' (1982), which uses Dm and C chords.

Three-chord songs

Many pop songs are based around three chords, the most common combination being the primary triads I, IV and V (see 'The three-chord trick', page 52). The **three-chord riff** is a repeated two-bar pattern that can be found across all song styles, from the intro to Hendrix's 'All Along The Watchtower' (1968): |C#m – – –| A – B –|| to 'Anarchy In The U.K.' by the Sex Pistols (1977): |C– – –| F – C –||.

> A **riff** is a short, repeated melodic pattern of usually two or four bars' duration. It can be adapted slightly during a song, e.g. with small changes to its shape or by being moved up or down in pitch.

The 12-bar blues

The 12-bar blues is based on three chords: the tonic (I), the subdominant (IV) and the dominant (V). The chords for the key of C are shown in brackets alongside the Roman numerals.

I (C)		**I** (C)		**I** (C)		**I** (C)	
IV (F)		**IV** (F)		**I** (C)		**I** (C)	
V (G)		**IV** (F) or V (G)		**I** (C)		**I** (C)			

Many variants on the above structure have been developed:

- Bar 2 often has chord IV in the place of chord I.
- Bar 12 may use chord V in place of chord I (the dominant chord tends to lead to the tonic so this helps to lead into the next verse).
- Some or all of the chords may be played as 7th chords (I[7], IV[7] and V[7]).

Four-chord patterns

Four-chord patterns are by far the most common chord progressions and are usually four bars long (with one chord per bar). Some four-chord patterns have been used so many times in songs that they can be considered 'stock progressions'. In the following examples of stock progressions, all the chords are shown in the key of C.

- **I–V–VI–IV (C–G–Am–F)**
  Someone Like You – Adele (2011)
  Let It Be – the Beatles (1970)
  Dammit – Blink 182 (1997)

- **I–VI–IV–V (C–Am–F–G)**
  This is sometimes known as the 'doo-wop' or '50s' progression because of its popularity during that decade.
  Stand By Me – Ben E King (1961)
  Jesus Of Suburbia – Green Day (2005)
  Unchained Melody – The Righteous Brothers (1965)
  I Will Always Love You – Dolly Parton (1974)

  > Doo-wop is a style of vocal R&B music using nonsense syllables that was popular with a cappella groups such as the Platters and the Coasters in the 1950s.

- **I, III, IV, V (C, Em, F, G)**
  Notice that the last three chords of this progression create an ascending bass line when played in root position.
  Crocodile Rock (verse) – Elton John (1972)
  I Feel Fine (chorus) – the Beatles (1964)
  Changes (chorus) – David Bowie (1971)

- **VI, IV, I, V, (Am, F, C, G)**
  Poker Face – Lady Gaga (2008)
  Self Esteem – The Offspring (1994)
  Not Afraid – Eminem (2010)

Eight-bar chord patterns

Some songs are based on longer eight-bar chord patterns. The **circle of fifths** (see next page) sometimes forms the basis of eight-bar chord patterns.

- 'Hey Joe' (1965) by Jimi Hendrix uses an eight-bar chord pattern that starts with an ascending circle of fifths: C–G–D–A–E–E–E–E.

- Lou Reed's song 'Perfect Day' (1972) uses a descending circle of fifths as its eight-bar chord pattern: Am–D–G–C–F–Bdim–E–E.

Another eight-bar chord progression is the 8-bar blues, where the chord structure of the 12-bar blues is adapted to fit into eight bars.

- 'Heartbreak Hotel' (1956) by Elvis Presley is one such example, following a I–I–I–III–IV–IV–V–I pattern.

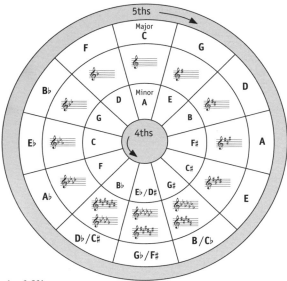

The circle of fifths

Modulation (the 'key change')

When a piece of music changes key it is said to 'modulate'. In pop music, this is referred to as the **key change** and is often used in power ballads. Key changes:

- are usually between keys that are closely related to one another, such as the dominant, the subdominant and the relative minor or major.

- serve to add energy to a song and are often used towards the close, acting as a climax.

- often move 'upwards' to the new key, with the melody sung at a higher pitch; this brings a sense of renewed energy to the music. 'Downward' modulations are rarer.

- are often introduced by moving from the dominant to the tonic of the new key to form a **perfect cadence** (see page 60).

There are various ways of changing key:

1. An **abrupt modulation** describes a sudden, unprepared move into a new key. A common device in pop music is to raise the key by a tone or semitone for the last verse or chorus; this gives a sense of climax and allows the singer to hit higher notes. Michael Jackson's 'Man In The Mirror' (1987) features an abrupt semitone key change at the repeat of the final chorus.

2. A **pivot chord** is a chord common to both keys and can be used to smooth out the modulation. For example, G can act as a pivot chord when modulating from C major to D major:

> **Pivot chord**
> V of C major
> IV of D major
> ↓
> C–F–Dm–Em–F–**G**–A7–D

3. The **circle of fifths** (see page 66) can be used to modulate, with the root notes moving upwards or downwards in fifths until arriving at the desired key.

4. A sequence of **descending parallel chords** can lead the music into a new key, e.g. F–Em–E♭–Dm–G

> Parallel chords keep the same shape from one chord to the next, so that the lines move in parallel. For example, a chord of F, A and C would be parallel to a chord of E, G and B.

Arranging chords

How chords are arranged helps to bring variety and interest to a song. There are many ways to vary how chords are used, including the voicing of individual chords, the rhythms used and the choice of chord layout or figuration. When arranging chords, it is important not only to consider the musical effect that is created but also the capabilities and limitations of the instrument(s) being used (see 'Instruments and Voices' chapter, page 103).

Chord voicing

This refers to how the individual notes within chords are arranged. **Chord inversions** (or **slash chords**) are ways to vary the voicing by using a note other than the root as the bass of some chords (see page 53). Other common types of chord voicing are **closed** and **open** position chords:

Closed and open position

When a triad is arranged with all its notes close together, it is said to be in **closed position**:

Closed position

> Notes in a closed position triad are arranged within one octave span.

When a triad is arranged with its notes spaced out, it is said to be in **open position**:

Open position

> Notes in an open position chord are arranged over more than one octave span.

Theory in practice: chord voicing for keyboards and guitar

There are many different ways of voicing a chord. Here is the chord of C voiced in three ways for keyboards, with the bass note (the root) in the left hand:

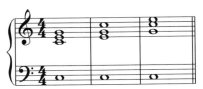

Guitar chords can be played in several positions. The aim should be to make the chords flow from one to the other without the parts leaping about, as in the following example:

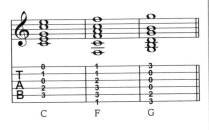

Rhythm

Distinctive rhythms can add interest to block chord arrangements:

Example of a distinctive rhythm

The Kinks' song 'All Day And All Of The Night' (1987) is built upon a simple sliding power chord riff, but is given a distinct sound by the use of a characteristic rhythm.

Chord layout

Rather than always being arranged as blocks, with all notes sounding together, chords can be broken up or used as repeated phrases or **figurations**; this is a simple way to bring variety and interest to a song accompaniment.

A **broken chord** is a term for when the notes of a chord are sounded individually. Here are some commonly used broken-chord figurations:

The intro to 'Everybody Hurts' (1992) by R. E. M. uses broken chords in this shape.

Radiohead's song 'Creep' (1993) uses a similar kind of broken-chord figuration.

An **arpeggio** is a type of broken chord in which the notes are played in order, from the lowest to the highest or vice versa:

> Elton John typically uses a mixture of block chords and broken chords in his piano parts.

Passing notes

Passing notes can add variety and decoration to the harmonic structure of music. They do not form part of the chord but are added between harmonising notes as decoration. They are so called because they pass from one note to another. In the following example, the right hand moves between the harmonies through a descending scalic passage; passing notes are indicated by a *:

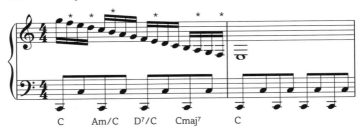

Transposition

'Being able to hear a melody or chord progression, and then play or sing it starting on any given note, is one of the most useful skills a musician can acquire. The ability then to write down a piece of music in any key will add another string to your bow, allowing you and others to play it on a diverse range of instruments.'

Paul Harris

Introducing transposition

Transposition is the process of writing or performing music at a higher or lower pitch than the original. When a song is transposed, all the notes are raised or lowered by the same interval. Rock and pop musicians are often called upon to play a song in a key other than the original. A key change may be needed because:

- the singer finds the melody in the original key too high or too low for their vocal range
- a song is more suitable for a particular instrument in a different key
- a song or part is written or played on a transposing instrument.

Transposition shortcuts

The easiest way to change key on a guitar is by using a **capo.** The capo is a device placed on the neck of the instrument that works by shortening the strings to raise the pitch of the notes. This means that the same chord fingerings in one key can be used to play in a different key. Guitarists can also **de-tune** their instrument down by a semitone or tone. Most music-notation software programmes have a transposition tool that can be a useful time-saver. Although these shortcuts may be used, it is useful to understand how the process of transposition works.

Transposing at the octave

The most straightforward transposition is at the octave; this means transposing notes either up or down by the interval of an octave. With octave transposition, the note names, key signature and any accidentals remain the same as the original score:

Upper octave

Middle octave

Lower octave

A melody written at three different octaves

In the above example, the lowest octave transposition has been written in the bass clef; this means that the notes fit within the stave, making the music easier to read.

C written at three different octaves on a piano keyboard staff

Transposing chords into another key

When chords are transposed into a different key, they still maintain their original character: a major chord is still a major chord; a minor chord remains minor, etc. Thus:

Chord sequence in C:	C	Am	Em	F	G7	C
	↓	↓	↓	↓	↓	↓
Chord sequence in D:	D	Bm	F♯m	G	A7	D

Theory in practice: transposing chord sequences

The first step when transposing chord sequences is to establish the original key. To do this you need to:

- look out for home (tonic) chords (see page 50)
- look out for cadence points (see page 60)
- check that all the chords belong to the key (see page 36).

Example: The chord sequence C Am Em F G7 C is in C major.

✔ The sequence starts and ends on a C major triad

✔ G7–C forms a perfect cadence in C major

✔ All of the chords belong to the key of C major.

Once you have established the original key, you can use either of these methods to transpose the chord sequence:

Method 1 Transpose the letter names of the chords up or down by the required interval (see page 24) into the new key.

- Work out the interval between the original key and the key of transposition.
- Work out the key signature of the new key.
- Transpose each chord up or down by the required interval.

Example: transposing into D major

✔ D is a major 2nd higher than C, so each of the chords needs to be a major 2nd higher.

✔ D major has two sharps: F♯ and C♯

The transposed chord sequence is: D Bm F♯m G A7 D

Method 2 Transpose the degrees of the scale (see page 34) of the original sequence into the new key.

- Work out which degrees of the scale the original chords are formed on.
- Find these degrees of the scale in the new key.

Example: transposing into D major

✔ C D E F G A B = I II III IV V VI VII

✔ I II III IV V VI VII = D E F♯ G A7 B C♯

The transposed chord sequence is: D Bm F♯m G A7 D

Transposing melodies into another key

When transposing music up or down by an interval other than an octave, the key signature of the music will change. The following passage from Lee Grabbe's *Calico Rag* (1905) is in F major (with a key signature of one flat):

To transpose this passage up by a major 2nd, a key signature of G major (one sharp) is needed in order to produce the same pattern of intervals:

Similarly, in order to transpose this passage down by a perfect 5th, a key signature of B♭ major is needed:

Any accidentals used against specific notes in the original score need to be reflected in the transposition. For instance, the F♯ in the original passage above becomes G♯ or B♮ in the transposed scores.

Theory in practice: transposing melodies

Transposing into another key

Once you have established the key of the original score, count up or down from the key-note by the required interval to find the new key and key signature. Next, write down the first note – there are several ways to work out the notes that follow:

1 Transpose each of the original notes in turn by the required interval, e.g. when transposing up by a major 2nd:

OR

2 Work out the degrees of the scale for each note in the original key, and then find equivalent notes in the new key:

OR

3 Follow the shape of the melody, imitating the pattern of intervals from one note to the next:

Theory in practice: transposing checklist
- Have you included the correct clef, key signature and time signature?
- Is your first note correct? When transposing at the octave, make sure you have written it at the new octave and not at the same pitch or two octaves lower or higher.
- Have you included all accidentals in the original score that were used outside of the key signature?
- Are the intervals between every note exactly the same as the original? Take particular care on notes with accidentals.
- If transposing between bass clef and treble clef, make sure the notes that were in spaces in the original score are now on the lines, and vice versa.

Transposing parts into the alto or tenor clef

When writing for string instruments, it is sometimes necessary to transpose a passage from the treble or bass clef into the alto or tenor clef (see page 20). Viola parts, for instance, are largely written in the alto clef but occasionally use the treble clef for higher notes; similarly cello parts are mostly written in the bass clef but also use the tenor clef for the higher part of their range.

When transposing from one clef to another, it helps to know where middle C is placed on each of the clefs:

The relative position of middle C in each clef

Transposing instruments

Transposing instruments are those instruments whose notes are written at a different pitch from the pitch they produce when played. The pitch at which they 'sound' is called **concert pitch**.

> - When a trumpet in Bb plays a written C, a Bb is sounded.
> - When an alto saxophone in Eb plays a written C, an Eb is sounded.

In the following passage, all three instruments produce the melody at the same concert pitch, even though they are written differently:

> There are various reasons why transposing instruments are used, but they largely relate to making the music more straightforward for the performer to read and play. This was particularly the case for some instruments in their early stages of development.

Writing for the horn section

Horn sections are commonly found in funk, ska, soul, R&B, jazz and swing bands. Sometimes the horn section improvises simple backing parts; at other times parts are written for them by an arranger. The horn section of a band includes transposing instruments. A typical horn section is made up of saxophone (transposing), trumpet (transposing) and trombone but sometimes other instruments are added such as flute, clarinet (transposing) or flugelhorn (transposing).

Instrument	Written/ Sounds	Interval	In order to sound in C major, the key signature must be:
Clarinet in B♭		Major 2nd lower	D major
Bass clarinet		Major 2nd + octave lower	D major
Soprano saxophone		Major 2nd lower	D major
Alto saxophone		Major 6th lower	A major
Tenor saxophone		Major 2nd + octave lower	D major
Baritone saxophone E♭		Minor 6th + octave lower	A major
Flugelhorn		Major 2nd lower	D major
French horn in F		Perfect 5th lower	G major
Trumpet in B♭		Major 2nd lower	D major

Transposing instruments found in the horn section

Famous funk horn sections include: Average White Band, Kool and the Gang, Tower of Power, Chicago and The JB Horns (James Brown's horn section). One of the most well-known today is the Miami Horns, who support Bruce Springsteen and Southside Johnny and the Asbury Dukes.

Octave transposition

When the range of an instrument is too high or too low for the music to be easily written on bass or treble clef, it may be notated an octave lower or higher than the sounding pitch, in order to reduce the number of ledger lines. The double bass, guitar, banjo and bass flute all sound an octave lower than written.

Score reading and writing

' 'Follow the signs to the shops', 'No right turn', 'Click to post your message' … The world is full of terms and signs. We need to know what they mean, otherwise things don't happen (or we end up in the wrong place!). Musical terms and signs are useful 'abbreviations' for conveying information: much can be communicated with a word or symbol.'

Paul Harris

The score

The written form of a musical composition is known as a **score**. A full score includes parts for all of the instruments, while a short score includes only the most important elements. The types of short score most commonly used in pop music are the **lead sheet** and the **PVG** (piano, vocal and guitar arrangement).

Lead sheet

As many rock and pop musicians don't read music notation, it is increasingly common just to provide lyrics and chords as a way of documenting songs; this means you don't have to be a music reader to play. Lead sheets take different formats, but most include the following elements:
- The melody of any intro, break or ending
- The full lyrics and vocal line
- Chord names or symbols
- An indication of the tempo and feel

PVG (Piano/Vocal/Guitar)

A PVG includes the following parts:
- piano part with an arrangement of the band parts
- vocals – melody and lyrics
- guitar symbols (usually chord boxes) above the stave

To write for guitar, you should include vocal line and lyrics, standard stave notation, chord names and tablature (see page 147).

Theory in practice: score layout

There are few strict rules regarding score layout for rock and pop music. However, when you are creating a full score, it is advisable to:
- write at the top of the title page the names of the composer or songwriter, the lyricist and the arranger (if there is one)
- put the tempo and feel of the song over the top of the first bar
- make sure the layout is clear to read
- group instruments together into families (a bracket or brace can be used to link them).

continued

Decide whether you are going to write the score at concert pitch or as a transposing score. A **score at concert pitch** is written in the key that the music sounds. A **transposing score** is sometimes used for 'transposing instruments' – where the key that is written down is actually different from the key produced when the instrument is played. Either is fine, but you will need to be careful with transposition when you are creating the score (see 'Transposition', page 71).

Tempo indications

Tempo markings indicate the speed at which the music should be played. They can be shown by metronome markings, beats per minute (bpm) and/ or directions given in words.

A **metronome** is a device that marks time by measuring the number of regularly recurring beats that occur within a minute. This gives players an exact indication of the tempo required.

♩ = 60 indicates a speed of 60 crotchet beats per minute.

♩. = 54 indicates a speed of 54 dotted-crotchet beats per minute.

The metronome was patented by Johann Nepomuk Maelzel in 1815.

Tempo markings describe the speed and sometimes the character of the music, e.g. 'fairly fast', 'slow ballad' or 'light folk feel'.

Tempo changes

Sometimes songwriters wish to speed up or slow down the tempo of a section of music. In rock and pop music, **half-time feel** is a very common tempo marking that literally means the music moves to half the speed of the previous tempo. There is an example of this in 'I Knew You Were Trouble' (2012) by Taylor Swift.

Dynamic markings

The word 'dynamics' is used to describe the varying degrees of loudness and softness at which music can be performed. Although many performance indications in popular music are given in English (such as tempo markings) dynamics are usually written in Italian. Here is a list of the most frequently used dynamic markings:

Abbreviation/sign	Italian term	Meaning
mf	*mezzo forte*	moderately loud
f	*forte*	loud
ff	*fortissimo*	very loud
mp	*mezzo piano*	moderately quiet
p	*piano*	quiet
pp	*pianissimo*	very quiet
cresc.	*crescendo*	getting louder
decresc,	*decrescendo*	getting quieter
dim.	*diminuendo*	getting quieter
◁	*crescendo*	getting louder
▷	*diminuendo*	getting quieter

◁   ▷   These signs are sometimes known as hairpins.

Qualifying terms

Tempo and dynamic markings can be qualified by the addition of the following Italian terms:

Italian term	Meaning	Example
meno	less	*meno mosso* (less movement, slower)
molto	much, very	*cresc. molto* (gradually get much louder)
più	more	*più mosso* (more movement, quicker)
poco a poco	little by little	*poco a poco cresc.* (get louder little by little)
sempre	always	*sempre forte* (always loud)
subito (or *sub.*)	suddenly	*subito* **pp** (suddenly very quiet)

Tempo and expression marks were developed into a system between 1600 and 1750, when Italian music dominated the European scene.

Articulation signs

Slurs (⌒ or ⌣) are used to link two or more consecutive notes together. Notes that are slurred should be played *legato* (i.e. smoothly, without any gaps between them) and are positioned above or below the relevant notes. In the following passage, the consecutive quavers are slurred together and should therefore be played *legato*:

A ⌒ between two notes is also used to indicate a hammer on and pull off (see page 87).

Phrases are subdivisions of the melodic line and are shown by a type of slur called a **phrase mark**. Notes that appear within a phrase mark should be played in a smooth and connected manner. In the following passage, the melody is subdivided into two-bar phrases:

Sometimes a comma (ˏ) is written above the stave between phrases; this indicates a breath mark (for singers and wind players) or a slight pause for other instrumentalists.

Dots placed above or below the notes should be played ***staccato*** – short, light and detached:

Horizontal dashes placed above or below the notes should be played ***tenuto*** – slightly stressed and then held on for their full value:

Accented notes are marked with an arrow head (>) placed above or below the note head. They should be played with emphasis and a short attack:

The *fermata*

A **pause** or ***fermata*** (⌢) placed over or under a note or rest means that the note or rest should be prolonged. The length of the pause is at the discretion of the performer:

G.P. is short for '**general pause**' and indicates that all performers should be silent, usually for one or two bars.

> The Foo Fighters use a **G.P.** in between the intro and the verse of their song 'Monkey Wrench' (1997).

When the abbreviation **8va** or **8** is written *above* notes, they should be performed an octave higher than written. This reduces the number of ledger lines and makes the music easier to read.

Two-bar phrase written using 8va and at sounding pitch.

Likewise, **8vb** is written *below* notes, they should be performed an octave lower than written:

The dashed line indicates the passage that should be played at the higher octave.

Articulation signs and techniques for guitar and bass

Here are some of the most common articulation signs used in guitar music:

Hammer on: a technique where two ascending notes on the string are sounded, but the string is only plucked once. This is indicated by a ⌒

Pull off: a technique where two descending notes are sounded, but the string is only plucked once. This is indicated by a ⌒

Slide: the fretting hand is used to slide smoothly up or down to the next note – the combination of a ⌒ and ⟋ shows that this is a slide.

Bending notes: the string is bent to raise the pitch of a note. There are several different types of bends that relate to how far the pitch is altered; these include the **half-step**, **whole-step** and **quarter-tone bends**. The example below uses a whole-step bend followed by half-step bend and two further whole-step bends:

Muted strings: the use of cross note-heads (**x**) indicates notes that should be muted to produce a percussive sound. The effect is created by laying the fretting hand across all six strings while the pick hand strikes a specific area – low, middle or high.

Palm mute: here the notes are muted with the strumming hand – the sound is deadened but the pitches can still be heard. This technique is commonly found in rock guitar music, e.g. in 'Doctor Feelgood' (1989) by Mötley Crüe and 'Run On The Hills' (1982) by Iron Maiden.

Harmonics: also known as '**overtones**', harmonics are high-pitched notes with a different, 'silvery' sound quality. They are produced by lightly touching the string over certain frets. Harmonics are shown by the use of diamond note-heads:

Whammy bar (or '**tremolo arm**'): a device that can produce a range of effects – pushing the arm down lowers the pitch of the note and pulling the arm up raises it.

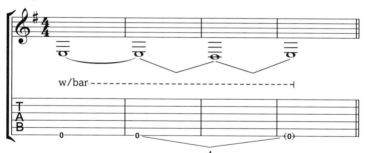

Vibrato: the regular, rapid fluctuation of pitch that can be used to add warmth and expression to a note. There are several ways of producing guitar *vibrato*, using either the fretting hand or a whammy bar. The most commonly used method is to rock the fingertip rapidly from side to side. *Vibrato* is shown by wavy lines above the notes in question.

Repeat signs: section repeats

When a whole section of music is repeated, it is often clearest to use repeat signs (‖: :‖) rather than writing out the same music twice. Repeat signs should be placed at the beginning and the end of the section to be repeated:

> If a repeated section begins at the very start of a piece, the opening repeat sign is not needed.

If a section is played twice, but with a different ending on the repeat, you will need to use **first-** and **second-time endings**.

> First- and second-time endings can last longer than one bar and do not have to be the same length as each other. Sometimes pieces use multiple endings.

In the previous example, the section under ⌐1.⌐ should be played the first time through; on the repetition, the section under ⌐2.⌐ should be played instead. This is how it would be written out in full:

Da Capo and *Dal Segno* repeats

Da Capo al Fine (or '**D.C. al Fine**') means repeat from the beginning and end at the word 'Fine'.

Da Capo al Coda (or '**D.C. al Coda**') means repeat from the beginning and end by playing the **Coda** (the closing section of a movement or piece).

Dal Segno al Fine (or '**D.S. al Fine**') means repeat from the 𝄋 sign and end at the word 'Fine'.

Dal Segno al Coda (or '**D.S. al Coda**') means repeat from the 𝄋 sign and end by playing the Coda.

Passage showing a 𝄋 sign

When Dal segno repeats are used, you have to locate the 𝄋 sign earlier on in the piece.

Repetition of bars

The sign ℀ means repeat the previous bar:

The sign  means repeat the previous two bars:

Similar signs can be used for different numbers of bars.

Repetition of ♪s, ♪s and ♪s

One **slash** through the stem of a note, or above or below a semibreve, tells the performer to play **quavers** up to the value of that note:

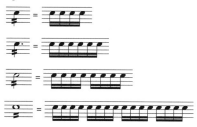

Two slashes tells the performer to play **semiquavers** up to the value of that note:

In the same way, three slashes means play demisemiquavers up to the value of that note.

Repetition of pairs of notes

Patterns of alternating notes can be shown by beaming the two notes and placing a short dash inside the beam:

Very fast repetitions of individual or alternating notes create a particular effect known as **tremolo**; composers usually add '*tremolo*' or '*trem.*' when this effect is required.

Word setting

The way in which words are set to music is key to creating an effective song. Words can be taken from existing songs or texts, or may be written specially for the music. When words are set to music:

• each syllable is placed directly under the appropriate note.

• hyphens are used between syllables of the same word.

Extract from 'Raggle Taggle Gypsy' (folk song)

Word setting may be **syllabic** (with one note sung to a syllable) or **melismatic** (with more than one note sung to a syllable); melismas are characteristic of urban R&B music and are widely used by singers such as Mariah Carey and Whitney Houston.

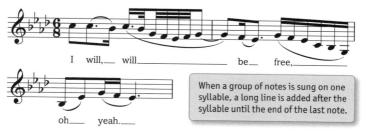

> When a group of notes is sung on one syllable, a long line is added after the syllable until the end of the last note.

Use of melisma

Word painting

In order to bring out the mood and meaning of lyrics, songwriters sometimes use a device known as word painting, where the text content is reflected in the music. This is found in songs of all styles and genres. For instance:

- Several songs by the Arctic Monkeys, including the opening of 'Dancing Shoes' (2006).
- The Motown Holland-Dozier-Holland song 'How Sweet It Is To Be Loved By You' (1964) uses word painting for the words 'I wanna stop …': the music stops at this point, before the lyrics continue with '… and thank you, baby'.
- In the folk song 'Raggle Taggle Gypsy' (above), the word 'high' is set at a higher pitch than the word 'low'. This is a commonly used example of word painting and one that George Michael uses to great effect in the Wham song 'Wake Me Up Before You Go-Go' (1984).

Theory in practice: word setting

When setting words to music, it is important to bring out their mood and meaning. Therefore, every aspect of the melody needs to be devised with the words in mind – from the tempo, metre and rhythm to the tonality, melodic shape and dynamics.

- Read the words out loud – the rhythm of the words may suggest strong and weak beats and thus duple, triple or quadruple time
- Choose a tempo that supports the delivery of the text
- Think about which words are naturally stressed or warrant more emphasis, and create a rhythm that complements this.
- Consider the phrasing and shape of the melody; are there places where you would like the melody to rise or fall?
- If you write down your song, make sure that each syllable comes directly under the appropriate note, and use hyphens between syllables of the same word.

Forms and structural devices

'Songs and pieces come in all shapes and sizes: long, short, repetitive, contrasting, solid, floaty … What all pieces have in common, however, is an overarching musical structure or form: many pop songs, for instance, are developed around a verse and chorus structure, where two melodic ideas alternate with each other. By giving music a coherent structure, you are transforming it from a collection of discrete and maybe disconnected musical elements into an articulate and unified musical work.'

Paul Harris

12-bar blues

The 12-bar blues is one of the most commonly used forms in popular music. Made up of three four-bar phrases, each with a line of lyrics, it is built on three chords: the **tonic** (chord I), the **subdominant** (chord IV) and the **dominant** (chord V). Here is the most common blues chord sequence:

I	I	I	I
IV	IV	I	I
V	IV	I	I

In the key of C this would be:

C	C	C	C
F	F	C	C
G	F	C	C

> The 12-bar blues is found in R&B, rock 'n' roll and jazz music as well as the blues.

Variants

There are many ways that the classic 12-bar blues sequence can be varied:

- Individual chords can be substituted:
  - In bar 2, chord I can be replaced with chord IV.
  - In bar 10, chord IV can be replaced with chord V.
  - In bar 12, chord I can be replaced with chord V.

> When chord V is used in the last bar, this gives the verse a natural tendency to lead into the next verse, since chord V (the dominant) tends to lead to chord I (the tonic or key-note). It is sometimes called a **turnaround** because it is leading into the next section.

- All chords can be played as 7ths:

I^7	I^7	I^7	I^7
IV^7	IV^7	I^7	I^7
V^7	IV^7	I^7	V^7

- The number of bars in each phrase can be increased in order to create longer blues sequences, e.g. the 24-bar blues.

Lyric structure

The words of a blues song are often concentrated in the first half of each line, allowing a guitar (or other instrument) break or fill before the next line. Structurally, the second line is usually a repeat of the words of first line.

This is followed by a different third line that may act as a response to – or even a punchline for – what came before:

> I'm gonna get up in the morning, believe I'll dust my broom.
>
> I'm gonna get up in the morning, believe I'll dust my broom.
>
> Girl, that man you been lovin', he can have my room.
>
> *'I Believe I'll Dust My Broom' by Robert Johnson*

Verse and chorus form

The most commonly used structure in pop music is verse and chorus, where a song is built around two alternating sections of melody – the **verse** and the **chorus**.

The **verse** is sung several times to different words.

- The melody and chord progression are the same each time.
- The lyrics of the verses often have a storyline.
- Verses are interspersed with repetitions of the chorus.

The **chorus** is a setting of the refrain of the lyrics and usually returns several times.

- The words, melody and chord progressions are the same each time.
- The chorus lyrics often contain the title words of the song.
- This is normally the catchiest part of the song, sometimes containing the 'hook'
- Typically the chorus follows after one or two verses.

Variants

Verse and chorus form is often extended to include some or all of the following: intro (introduction), bridge, pre-chorus, *ad lib.* section, instrumental and coda and/or fade out.

- An **intro** is an opening section designed to catch the attention of the listener. It could be a repeated riff, a few strummed guitar chords or an instrumental version of the verse or chorus. Sometimes it is a soundscape or a gradual build-up of layers of instruments.

- A **bridge** is a short passage of contrasting material that links together two sections. It is often (though not always) eight bars long and is thus sometimes referred to as the **middle eight**.

- A **pre-chorus** is a short transitional section that, as its name implies, leads into the chorus.

- An **instrumental** is a solo section, often improvised, that is usually based on the chords of the verse or chorus.

- An *ad lib.* passage is a free section, often at the end of a song, where the vocalist improvises music based on earlier material.

- An **outro** (or **coda**) is a concluding section that brings the song to a close. It might be an instrumental version of the verse or chorus – perhaps loud and definite; perhaps quiet and questioning. Sometimes layers are gradually taken away.

- A **fade out** is where the music gradually gets quieter, until disappearing altogether to bring the song to a close.

32-bar song form (AABA)

The 32-bar song form (or AABA) was most commonly used by songwriters in the first half of the twentieth century. Many standards of the 1930s and 1940s follow this structure, including 'I Got Rhythm' by George Gershwin and 'Over The Rainbow' by Harold Arlen.

This form consists of four eight-bar phrases that are built on two melodic ideas ('A' and 'B').

- The **A section** is the main section. Each A section is similar in melody but usually has different lyrics.

- The **B section** differs from the A section both musically and lyrically. It provides melodic, harmonic, rhythmic and/or textural contrast to 'A', presenting the listener with a change in mood in the song. It is often in a different key (usually the subdominant or the relative minor).

Verse	Verse	Bridge	Verse
A	A	B	A

> This form is also known as **ballad form** and **American popular song form**.

Variants

There are several variants on the AABA pattern: sometimes the number of bars in each section differs from the standard 8+8+8+8 format (e.g. 'Yesterday' by The Beatles) and sometimes the song is extended with the addition of other sections such as an instrumental or a bridge (e.g. 'Every breath you take' by The Police).

32-bar verse	10-bar middle section	32-bar verse	Coda and fade out
A A B A	C (new material)	A A B A	based on A

Extended ABBA form, as used in 'Every Breath You Take' by The Police

Strophic form

This form is based on a series of verses without a chorus. While relatively rare in popular music, it is commonly found in folk song. The structure of strophic form can be shown using letter names as follows:

A A A A   *(etc. for further verses)*

> 'The House Of The Rising Sun' by the Animals uses strophic form, as do several of Rod Stewart's songs including 'Maggie May' with its 24-bar melody.

Dance music

The vast majority of dance music is in $\frac{4}{4}$. Tracks are built from interlocking layers of samples and loops, with every section being divisible by four bars; this means that sections typically last for 8, 16, 24 or 32 bars.

Sections

Although there are no set forms for dance tracks, each can be broken down into identifiable sections. Some dance tracks, such as 'Dirty Beats' by Roni Size, loosely follow a verse and chorus structure. The main sections of dance music can usually be defined as one of the following:

- The **intro**: a short section, usually 8 or 16 bars long. This is the opening passage in which the DJ mixes the previous track into the new one. The music is usually quite sparse, using a drum or percussion section and perhaps some short synth stabs or vocals.

- The **main section**: where the various elements that make up the track are combined in different ways, with instruments often dropping in and out of the mix. There are often brief drum and vocal-only episodes that serve to break up the structure.

- The **breakdown**: where layers of sounds drop out. This helps to create tension when the sounds are built back up again.

- The **reprise** of the **main section**: usually the climax of the track.

- The **outro**: the closing section in which the DJ starts to mix in the next track. Like the intro, the music is usually quite sparse; a common technique is to cut out the bass and then slowly fade out the main synth or vocal, keeping the drums going until the end.

Here is the structure of a classic dance song: 'Renegade Master' (Fatboy Slim Old Skool Mix) by Wildchild (1998):

Intro (mix in)	Main section	Breakdown	Reprise of main section	Outro (mix out)
32 bars	84 bars	36 bars	16 bars	18 bars

Instruments and voices

'In addition to rhythm, melody, harmony and form, we have a multitude of instruments, sounds and voices, each offering a unique sound-quality. And when used in combination, these sound-makers provide us with an infinite kaleidoscope of sonic possibility.'

Paul Harris

The guitar family

The guitar has a long history that goes back to well before the earliest surviving instruments of the sixteenth century. During the seventeenth century, the guitar was being played all over Europe; at this time it was a small, quiet instrument with four or five courses of gut strings. Larger acoustic guitars with six strings were introduced in the eighteenth century and were soon to dominate folk and popular music all over the world.

In the early twentieth century, the acoustic guitar was already an important instrument in blues and jazz, but by the 1920s guitarists in jazz bands found it difficult to be heard over the drums and powerful brass sections. Various instrument makers experimented with new designs to overcome this, and in 1936 Gibson produced the ES150 – the world's first successful Spanish-style electric guitar. In 1951 Fender's 'Precision' bass guitar offered an amplified bass to compete with the volume of drum-kits and amplified guitars. More than any other instrument, the electric guitar defines popular music.

> A course on a stringed instrument refers to two or more adjacent strings, usually played together and tuned in unison or an octave apart.

Sound production

All guitars use the same basic means of sound production: strings are stretched across a wooden body and are made to vibrate by being plucked. Different pitches are produced by changing the length of the string: the shorter the string, the higher the note. The length of a string is reduced by the player pressing it down with the fingers on different places on the fingerboard. The fingerboard is divided into semitones by means of frets.

There are several basic ways to play the guitar:
* Strumming with or without a plectrum (or pick)
* 'Finger style', where individual strings are picked out
* With a bottleneck – a metal tube placed over the finger to produce a sliding *glissando* effect.

Acoustic guitar

The acoustic guitar has a hollow, usually wooden, body with six strings tuned to E A D G B E (from low to high) that span two octaves. The sound is produced by the vibration of the strings and is amplified through the resonating hollow body of the instrument.

Open strings on the acoustic guitar   *Normal range of the acoustic guitar*

The acoustic guitar sounds an octave lower than written.

There are various kinds of acoustic guitar:

- The **nylon-strung guitar** is soft-toned and usually played finger style. It is mainly used in Classical, Latin American and Spanish music.
- The **steel-strung guitar** is brighter and louder, but still needs amplification to play in a band.
- The **twelve-string guitar** has double courses of strings that produce a rich, shimmering sound. Usually strummed, it is often used by blues players, notably Lead Belly and Blind Willie McTell.
- The **lap slide guitar** is a type of guitar where the player slides a piece of metal up and down the strings of their instrument, which is held flat on their lap.

Pop and rock guitarists usually improvise from chord symbols or read five-line TAB notation (see page 147).

Acoustic guitars usually need further amplification when playing with a band. This can be produced in two ways:

- With an in-built pickup, an electrical device that can be connected to an amplifier.
- By placing a microphone in front of the sound-hole of the guitar.

Notable acoustic guitarists
Classical: Julian Bream, Segovia, John Williams
Flamenco: Paco de Lucia, Paco Peña
Jazz, blues, pop and rock: Chet Atkins, Robert Johnson, John Martyn, John McLaughlin, Joni Mitchell, Laura Marling, Nick Mulvey, Django Reinhardt, James Taylor
Folk: Martin Carthy, Davey Graham, Bert Jansch, Richard Thompson
Slide guitar: Ry Cooder

Electric and bass guitar

Electric guitars and bass guitars normally have solid bodies and only work with an amplifier. The sound is produced by the vibration of the strings, which is then amplified electrically. The amplification can be produced in two ways:
- Using an amplifier connected to a speaker cabinet ('cab').
- Through a unit that combines both amplifier and speaker.

Electric guitar

The electric guitar performs one of two roles in a band (sometimes both).
- A **rhythm guitarist** has an accompanying role, mainly playing chords in combination with the bass and drums, together forming the rhythm section.
- A **lead guitarist** mainly plays single-note melodies and improvises solos. Like the acoustic guitar, the electric guitar has six strings that are tuned to E A D G B E (from low to high), spanning two octaves.

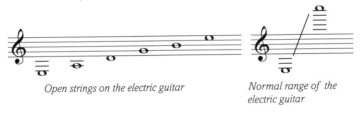

Open strings on the electric guitar

Normal range of the electric guitar

> The electric guitar sounds an octave lower than written.

Effects

Electric guitarists often use pedals, amplifiers, table-top units or rack mounts to vary the sound they produce; some of these may be built into their instruments. The combination of guitar, amp, speakers and effects is what gives individual players their distinctive sound. Common effects include:
- **Overdrive**: produced by slightly distorting the signal, e.g. the opening riff in Michael Jackson's 'Beat It' (1982)
- **Chorus**: the effect of many guitars playing at once, e.g. Nirvana's 'Come As You Are' (1991)

- **Reverb and echo/delay**: U2's guitarist, The Edge, often uses delay pedals, e.g. in 'Pride (In The Name Of Love)' (1984)
- **Wah-wah pedal**: this device continuously varies the tone of the guitar, producing vowel-like guitar sounds. It is famously used in Isaac Hayes' theme music to the seventies film *Shaft*, and by Jimi Hendrix on 'Voodoo Chile (Slight Return)' (1971)
- **Phaser**: a swirling sound, e.g. Van Halen's 'Eruption' (1978)
- **Fuzz box**: a fuzzy, distorted sound, e.g. Rolling Stones 'Satisfaction' (1965)

Electric guitar players usually improvise from chord symbols or read five-line TAB notation (see page 147).

> **Notable electric guitarists**
> Jeff Beck, Chuck Berry, Anna Calvi, John Frusciante, PJ Harvey, Jimi Hendrix, B B King, Jimmy Page, Carlos Santana, Ali Farka Toure, Joe Satriani, Steve Vai, Muddy Waters, Jack White

Bass guitar

The bass guitarist provides the harmonic and rhythmic foundation of the band: working with the drummer to provide a steady rhythm ('locking in with the drummer') and providing the bass line of the harmony. The bass part is usually a single-note line, played either by finger-picking or with a plectrum. Some pop styles – funk, for example – use a percussive **slap bass style** – striking the side of the thumb against the string (the 'slap'), then pulling the string away from the fingerboard and releasing it so that it slaps back against the fret board.

The bass guitar has four strings tuned to E A D G (from low to high), spanning an interval of a tenth. The strings sound an octave lower than the standard electric guitar.

Open strings on the bass guitar

Normal range of the bass guitar

> To avoid using too many ledger lines, the notes are written an octave higher than they sound.

There are a number of kinds of bass guitar:

* Some players use **fretless basses** that enable them to slide between notes more easily. The fretless bass has a less percussive sound.

* The **five-string bass** has an extended lower range, with an extra B string below the E string.

* The **six-string bass** has a high C string as well as a low B string, thus extending both the lower and higher range.

> One of the greatest exponents of the slap bass style is Mark King of Level 42.

The bassist often improvises from chord symbols or reads four-line TAB notation (five-line TAB for five strings, six-line TAB for six strings). For more detail, see page 147.

The double bass

The acoustic bass or double bass is found in some styles of pop music, notably rock and roll, blue grass and country. One of the most influential jazz double bass players was Charlie Mingus.

> Elvis Presley's bassist, Bill Black, was one of the first to use the electric bass when he played it on 'Jailhouse Rock' (1957).

> **Notable bass players**
> Bernard Edwards (Chic), John Entwistle (The Who), Flea (Red Hot Chili Peppers), James Jamerson (Motown), Geddy Lee (Rush), Jaco Pastorius, Suzi Quatro, Rhonda Smith (Prince, Jeff Beck), Victor Wooten

Drums and other percussion instruments

The drummer forms the backbone of the rhythm section, providing a steady beat and interlocking with the bass and rhythm guitars. Drum patterns are important in establishing the style of a song.

> **Notable drummers**
> Cindy Blackman (Lenny Kravitz), John Bonham, Billy Cobham, Sheila E., Steve Gadd, Clyde Stubblefield, Bernard Purdie (well known for his signature time pattern known as the 'Purdie Shuffle')

Drum kit

The drum kit provides the rhythmic foundation for a great deal of popular music. The standard kit is made up of:

- a **bass drum** or **kick drum**: played with a foot pedal (or a double pedal), it produces a low thumping sound. Some heavy rock bands use two bass drums

- a **snare drum**: played with drum sticks or wire brushes, the distinctive sound is produced by snare wires fitted to the underside of the drum that vibrate against the bottom drum skin

- one or more high **tom toms** and a low (floor) tom tom: these come in different sizes to produce different pitches. Some players have as many as eight – enough to produce a scale

- **cymbals**: played using sticks or brushes. The **splash** cymbal is used to play small crashes; the **crash** cymbal is thicker and heavier, and is used for more powerful accents; the **ride** cymbal is used to keep a steady beat.

- **hi-hat**: a pair of medium-sized cymbals mounted one above the other, played using sticks or brushes. They can also be played by using a foot pedal to open and close them

> American drummer Terry Bozio (Missing Persons and Frank Zappa) uses two octaves of pitched tom toms and several cymbals, bells and gongs to play melodic solos while accompanying himself with bass-note patterns.

Sound production

- Sticks are used to strike drums, causing the skin to vibrate and the drum shell to resonate and produce the sound. Sticks and mallets are available

in different weights and sizes, with different tips or heads. Brushes are
used to produce a quieter, swishy sound.

- Different sized drums produce different pitches: the larger the drum, the
  lower the pitch. The pitch of a drum may be altered by increasing or
  decreasing the tension of the skin with a drum key.

- Most contemporary drums have a drum skin on the underside of the
  shell; this produces additional resonance and can be tuned to alter the
  timbre of the drum.

Notation

Drummers normally improvise, establishing drum patterns and intersecting
them with breaks, licks and fills. However, drum parts can also be written
down using drum notation (see page 150).

> A fill is a short decorative solo that breaks the drum pattern.

> The drum break on the James Brown song 'Funky Drummer' (1970) is believed to
> have been sampled more than any other.

Electronic drums

Digital technology has opened the way for creating drum sounds in new ways:

- Many kits include electronic drum pads – flat pads that are played like a
  regular drum kit but using the sticks to trigger electronic drum sounds.

- Electronic triggers can be applied to acoustic drums, thus creating a
  'hybrid' of electronic and acoustic sounds.

- Digital drums are entirely electronic, with a set of drum pads mounted on
  a stand in a configuration similar to that of an acoustic drum kit layout.

Percussion

Drummers sometimes supplement their kit with percussion instruments
(instruments that are struck, shaken or rubbed). Here are some of the most
commonly used percussion instruments:

- **Congas** (large single-skinned drums) and **bongos** (small single-skinned
  drums) are free-standing instruments, usually in pairs, that are played
  with the hands

- The **tambourine**, a small drum with bells attached, may be struck, shaken or rubbed to produce different sounds
- The **triangle** is struck with a metal beater
- **Maracas** or **shakers** are gourds filled with beads that rattle when shaken
- A **woodblock** is a hollow box, played by striking with a wooden beater
- A **guiro** is a hollow box with ridges cut into it. It is played by scraping the ridged surface with a thin stick
- A **cowbell** is struck with a stick

Keyboard instruments

Bands use a wide range of keyboard instruments that can be broadly divided into pianos, organs, digital keyboards and synthesizers. Keyboards are very versatile and can perform several roles in a band, including:

- harmonising; playing chords
- playing lead lines and solos
- adding to the rhythm section
- providing or reinforcing the bass line
- providing sound effects using samples and effects pedals
- using synth pads to fill out the sound, e.g. brass and string sounds.

Range

Keyboards come in many sizes but usually have a range of at least five octaves. A full-size piano has a range of up to seven and a half octaves.

Notation

Keyboard players often improvise from chord symbols. However, written keyboard music follows conventional staff notation: two staves, one in treble clef for the right hand and the other in the bass clef for the left hand.

Conventional keyboard staff

Piano

The pianoforte, or piano for short, was invented around 1700. The sound is produced by hammering strings. When a key is pressed down, a felt-covered hammer hits the string (or strings); when released, a felt-covered damper is lowered to silence the sound. The piano is notoriously difficult to record, so digital keyboards are usually used in the recording studio.

Notable pianists and singer-songwriters
Pianists: Ray Charles, Chick Corea, Jamie Cullum, George Duke, Jerry Lee Lewis, Little Richard, Stevie Wonder, Joe Zawinul
Singer-songwriters: Kate Bush, Billy Joel, Elton John, Alicia Keys, Carole King, Nina Simone

Hammond organ

The Hammond organ has a unique sound and uses revolving discs to produce a variety of tone colours. When it went on the market in 1933, it was the first electronic keyboard instrument capable of playing more than one note at a time. It soon became popular in cinemas, theatres and dance bands (as well as American churches), and its soulful surging sound can be heard in gospel, jazz, psychedelia and garage rock, notably 'Gimme Some Lovin'' (1966) by the Spencer Davis Group.

Synthesizers

A synthesizer is a device that generates sounds electronically. The first synthesizer was developed in 1955 at the RCA studios in New York – it was huge and very expensive. In 1965 Robert A. Moog developed a smaller transistorized synthesizer, the **Moog** modular, which produced many sounds that could not be created on conventional instruments. The smaller **Minimoog** became the first portable integrated synthesizer.

In 1968, Walter Carlos recorded a collection of J. S. Bach's pieces played on the Moog (*Switched on Bach*), which sold over a million copies. Since then the Moog has featured on many songs and albums, notably the Beatles' *Abbey Road* (1969), *Autobahn* (1974) by Kraftwerk and Donna Summer's 1975 disco hit 'Love To Love You Baby'. Throughout the 1970s, ARP was in competition with Moog, with the analog ARP Odyssey being the main competitor to the Minimoog. In recent years highly realistic emulations of many models of classic synthesizers have become available.

Jean Michel Jarre played an ARP 2600 and an ARP sequencer on the album *Equinoxe* (1978).

Whereas a true synthesizer produces synthetic sounds by electronic means, the **Mellotron** played recordings of authentic instrumental sounds. The first Mellotron was built in 1963 – it was an early sample player, using tape loops. The unique sound of the Mellotron meant that it quickly became popular, being adopted by many bands including King Crimson, Led Zeppelin and the Moody Blues.

The German electronic music group Tangerine Dream used both the Moog and Mellotron in the 1960s and went on to pioneer synthesizer/sequenced electronic music.

The first commercially successful **digital synthesizer** was the Yamaha DX7, originally produced in 1983; it was used on many songs during the 1980s. As digital memory became cheaper and processors faster, synthesizers were able to have large numbers of samples on board. These could be processed through filters and special effects to produce both complex and realistic sounds. In the twenty-first century synthesizers are more powerful and easily affordable.

Notable synth players
Vince Clarke, Brian Eno, Pet Shop Boys

'Take On Me' (1985) by a-ha uses the iconic DX7 electric bass sound.

Digital keyboards

Nowadays digital keyboards use advanced synthesis technology, and they have much in common with synthesizers. However, the emphasis is not on the control of sound synthesis parameters: most feature hundreds of voices, styles and sounds; have touch-sensitive keys (the harder the key is pressed, the louder the sound); and include built-in mixers and sequencers, amplifiers and speakers. Many also have sound-editing capabilities and can be used as work stations for recording and composing.

Stage pianos are electronic keyboards designed to be used in live performances. They share some of the features of digital pianos and synthesizers but have a smaller number of sounds, a more robust body and often use external amplification.

Digital pianos have weighted keys that give an authentic piano feel. Nowadays it can be difficult to distinguish between the sound of a digital piano and the sound of an acoustic piano.

> **Notable keyboard players**
> Matt Bellamy, Keith Emerson, Jon Lord, Billy Preston, Rick Wakeman
>
> Matt Bellamy of Muse writes his songs at the piano, but when he plays on tour he uses a variety of synthesizers plus a digital stage piano encased in the shell of a grand piano.

Horn section

A typical horn section is made up of saxophone, trumpet and trombone but sometimes other instruments are added such as flute, clarinet or flugelhorn. Most of the instruments found in a horn section are transposing instruments, notably saxophones (in E♭ and B♭) and trumpet (in B♭) (see page 80).The main role of the horn section is to provide backing riffs and punctuations, such as accented stabs, along with a few written or improvised solos. The instruments are sometimes amplified using microphones when playing live.

> **Notable horn sections**
> Memphis Horns, Tower of Power

Saxophones

The saxophone uses a **single reed** – a thin flat piece of cane attached to the mouthpiece. The player's breath causes the reed to vibrate, which in turn sets the air column vibrating. Saxophones come in different sizes. The alto and tenor saxophones are the most common kinds, and saxophonists often double on flute and clarinet.

> One of the most famous alto saxophone solos was played by session musician Raphael Ravenscroft in the Gerry Rafferty song 'Baker Street' (1978). When the song was released, it led to an upsurge in saxophone sales.

Ranges

The saxophone has a normal range of about two and a half octaves, though players can reach higher notes. Here is the range of each instrument in the saxophone family.

| Soprano | Alto | Tenor | Baritone |

> **Notable saxophonists**
> King Curtis, John Coltrane, Jim Horn, Fela Kuti, Lenny Pickett, Barbara Thompson, Lee Thompson

Brass instruments

All brass instruments are made out of metal. Nowadays, however, they are more likely to be made out of mixed metals than pure brass. Going from highest to lowest pitch, the members of the brass family are: **trumpet**, **French horn**, **tenor trombone**, **bass trombone** and **tuba**. The French horn and tuba are not normally found in a horn section (see page 114).

> The melody at the beginning of the Beach Boys' song, 'God Only Knows' (1966) is played on a French horn.

Each brass instrument has a cup-shaped mouthpiece, a length of hollow tubing and a flared bell. The sound is produced by causing a column of air to vibrate inside a hollow tube. The vibrations are set up by the player's lips vibrating against the mouthpiece. Several notes can be sounded by the player simply altering the tension of their lips: the tighter the lips, the higher the pitch. To obtain more notes, either **valves** or a **slide** are used to alter the length of the tube. Both work on the same principle: the longer the tube, the lower the note.

Brass instruments may be played with a **mute** – a device, usually made out of metal or wood, that is inserted in the bell and alters the quality of the sound. Mutes come in different shapes and sizes, each producing a different distinctive *timbre*. Types include **cup**, **straight**, **Harman**, **plunger** and **bucket**.

Ranges

Here is the written range of each of the standard brass instruments. Some players may be able to play higher or lower than the notes given.

Trumpet   French horn

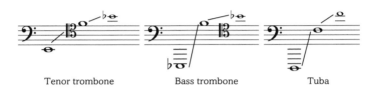

Tenor trombone   Bass trombone   Tuba

> The Youngblood Brass Band combines the traditional New Orleans brass-band sound with elements of hip hop, punk and jazz.

The **trumpet** is a **valve** instrument. Each of its three valves brings into action an extra length of tubing: when a valve is pressed down, an extra loop of tubing is added. The three valves can be used in different combinations to produce different pitches.

> A high-pitched trumpet in D is used in the Beatles' song 'Penny Lane' (1967).

> The Rizzle Kicks song 'Down With The Trumpets' (2011) features a mariachi trumpet sample. Mariachi is a type of Mexican folk music.

The **trombone** is a **slide** instrument that works by lengthening or shortening the instrument's tube. It was much used in early ska by bands such as the Skatalites and was later adopted by British ska bands such as The Specials. Notable trombone players include Don Drummond and Annie Whitehead.

The **tuba** was used on the earliest recordings of music. It was difficult to reproduce very low frequencies, which meant that string bass parts were sometimes doubled up on a tuba to make them audible. When microphones were introduced, the string bass could be more easily heard, and it soon supplanted the tuba.

Voices

The sound of the voice is produced by air being expelled from the lungs and vibrating the vocal cords – the tighter the vocal cords, the higher the note. The cavities in the throat, mouth, nose and head act as resonators to amplify and colour the sound.

Ranges and registers

- Most singers have a comfortable range of around one and a half octaves.
- The **head voice** and the **chest voice** are two distinct vocal registers. The chest voice is the lower register and has a more powerful tone, while the head voice is lighter and sits in the higher range.
- *Falsetto* is the vocal register above the one a voice naturally speaks or sings in.

Roy Orbison had a very wide range of about three octaves.

Falsetto was much used in male vocal groups in 1950s doo wop, then later in 1960s soul by artists such as The Temptations and Curtis Mayfield. A commonly used device in soul and disco is for the singer's voice to glide up to *falsetto* from the normal register; an example of this is the outro of 'Take On Me' (a-ha, 1985).

Notable *falsetto* singers include Prince, Michael Jackson, Justin Hawkins of the Darkness, Jónsi Birgisson of Sigur Rós, and Jimmy Somerville of Bronski Beat and the Communards. One of the best known *falsetto* songs is 'Smalltown Boy' (1984) by Bronski Beat.

Backing vocals

Backing vocals originated in the early days of gospel, where a large group of singers would respond to the soloist in a call-and-response style. Today they are used in much popular music and are usually sung by a small group of three or four singers. There are a number of ways that backing vocals can be used to fill out an arrangement, including:

- singing along with the lead singer
- using call and response
- using scat (nonsense) syllables
- singing wordless passages of 'oohs' and 'aahs'.

Styles and genres in popular music

' 'Variety is the spice of life.' This common saying could well be applied to music. Across the globe – and through the centuries – music has taken on a whole range of roles: purely as an art form, simply to be listened to and treasured; as a means of personal expression; a unifying social force; a tool for propaganda; an expression of status and stature. It's perhaps not surprising, then, that there is such a vast array of musical styles and genres around. In all likelihood, new styles will continue to be created for as long as we continue to create music!'

Paul Harris

Introduction and overview

What follows does not aim to be a comprehensive guide to all the major artists in popular music, but rather an overview of the musical characteristics found in prominent pop and rock styles looking at their origins and putting them into context.

Some artists and albums, although perhaps ground-breaking and influential, have a unique sound that does not belong within a particular genre; other major artists can be broadly classified as pop, rock, indie or singer-songwriters but do not fall into more closely defined genres.

Here are the main characteristics of these four loosely defined genres, which in themselves are umbrella terms for a huge range of styles. It should be noted that many musicians are not comfortable with these labels and resist categorisation, and others combine elements of more than one style across their careers (Stevie Wonder and Prince, for example).

Pop

The term 'pop music' was first used in the 1950s as a blanket term for music that is instantly appealing, chart-oriented and aimed at the teenage market. Pop music is often regarded as the softer alternative to rock, constituting songs that are relatively short and aimed at commercial recording. The basic elements of pop have remained fairly stable: the music is generally accessible and tends to focus on the vocals, with an emphasis on memorable hooks and catchy choruses. Pop music lyrics are often centred on romantic love.

> **Listening** ABBA, The Beach Boys, Britney Spears, Kylie Minogue, Michael Jackson, Robbie Williams, Spice Girls, Take That

Rock

The term 'rock music' was first used in the music press in the 1960s. Rock music is album-based and has splintered into many distinct subgenres over the years that are associated with particular subcultures. Rock music is typically guitar driven, played by bands with heavily amplified electric and bass guitars. Compared with pop, it considers itself less mainstream, more non-conformist and more profound.

> **Listening** Fleetwood Mac, The Killers, Kings of Leon, Led Zeppelin, Queen, Queens of the Stone Age, U2

Indie

During the 1960s the word 'alternative' was used to describe less commercially driven types of music, such as the ground-breaking albums by The Velvet Underground. Partly as an offshoot of the punk ethos, the word 'indie' became more widely used. The term is associated with small record labels (Rough Trade and Factory, for example) that are independent of the majors; these labels are perceived to be innovative, flexible and to favour 'authenticity' and artistic expression over commercial concerns. Indie music covers a range of styles, from grunge to the Madchester sound.

> **Listening** Arctic Monkeys, Cabaret Voltaire, The Fall, Happy Mondays, Joy Division, Morrissey, Muse, Radiohead, The Smiths, Stiff Little Fingers, Stone Roses

Singer-songwriters

Singer-songwriters both write and perform their material, usually accompanying themselves on acoustic guitar or piano. The folk music revival of the 1960s brought many singer-songwriters to prominence, notably Bob Dylan and Joan Baez, whose lyrics were often a form of protest. Singer-songwriters Joni Mitchell and James Taylor often sing about their personal experiences; the emphasis is often on the words and the music is usually lyrical, reflective and literate. The movement remained strong in the 1970s and onwards, and from the 1990s female singer-songwriters became increasingly prominent.

> **Listening** Kate Bush, Bob Dylan, Elton John, Jeff Buckley, Nick Drake, Simon and Garfunkel, Joni Mitchell, James Taylor, Neil Young, Tori Amos, Tracy Chapman, Suzanne Vega, Amy Winehouse, Adele

Origins of popular music

The origins of popular music are rooted in the USA and drawn from a mixture of African and European influences. New styles emerged when the music of black African slaves and white European settlers were fused together.

Ragtime

Ragtime is a style of syncopated piano music that originated in the saloons and brothels of the Southern States of the USA during the late nineteenth century. It is characterised by strongly syncopated melodies in the right hand and regularly accented accompaniments in the left hand. While the influence of African music can be heard in the use of syncopated rhythms, the structures and harmonies are akin to the European dance music of the time, particularly marches and waltzes.

> The son of a former slave, Scott Joplin (c.1867–1917) had a classical music training and was a key figure in ragtime. Famous Joplin rags include 'The Entertainer', 'Maple Leaf Rag' and 'The Easy Winners'.

Gospel

In the early nineteenth century, plantation owners tried to convert their slave workers to Christianity; this gave rise to a style of church music that combined the syncopations and polyrhythms of African music with European hymn tunes and harmonies. Gospel music emerged out of this tradition in the early twentieth century. Structurally, it was based on 'call and response', where a leader sings opening phrases (the 'calls') and the chorus of the congregation responds with shorter harmonised lines (the 'responses') – much like the backing vocals found in pop music. The black gospel style features melisma, where the same syllable is sung over several notes (see page 95).

> Gospel music has been hugely influential, particularly on soul music and R&B. Notable early gospel artists include The Staple Singers and Mahalia Jackson.

Early jazz

During the late nineteenth century, black marching bands were formed using European instruments (often leftovers from Civil War bands) but adapting them to their own traditions: introducing syncopated rhythms, bending notes and improvising jazzy new versions of the European march tunes. New Orleans was an important early centre of the development of this music and the place where jazz first became prominent. Eventually many jazz musicians travelled north, particularly to Chicago, in search of new work.

> Some of the earliest New Orleans-style jazz was recorded in the 1920s – notably by King Oliver's Creole Jazz Band. The Original Dixieland Jass Band made jazz popular with white audiences; their first recording, 'Dixieland Jazz Band One-Step/Livery Stable Blues', sold over a million copies.

Country music

Country music was rooted in the folk music brought by white settlers to the USA; most were very poor and lived in the Southern states. It absorbed and adapted many folk styles: narrative ballads, dances of various sorts, spirituals and blues. Jimmie Rodgers became country's first big recording star and record companies soon realised there was a large audience for 'hillbilly' music. In the early fifties, country songs started to make inroads into the pop charts; Hank Williams was its new star singer-songwriter. Other country styles included bluegrass, which continued the folk-dance traditions using fiddles, banjos, guitars and mandolins. Mainstream country music subsequently became highly commercialised and evolved into country and western, centring on the Nashville recording industry and the country radio stations (led by WSM's 'Grand Ole Opry').

The blues

Towards the end of the nineteenth century, African music was fused with the folk music of the white European settlers to produce new styles, including the blues. Early types of black American music were often based on call and response, such as spirituals (religious songs using vocal harmony) and work songs (songs that were sung in time with the task being done). The music was passed from musician to musician through oral tradition.

The early style of blues was known as 'country blues' and usually consisted of a solo singer accompanied on guitar, banjo or piano, sometimes with added harmonica or drums. When large numbers of people started to move to industrial cities in the early twentieth century, different styles of blues began to emerge; these are known collectively as '**city blues**' or '**urban blues**'.

Most blues songs feature:
- the 12-bar blues form (see page 98)
- four beats per bar
- a three-line verse structure, where the second line repeats the first: A A B
- raw, emotive lyrics dwelling on love and drink, and telling of injustice and hopelessness.

Many blues songs include a short instrumental break (solo) after each line – a sort of call and response.

> **Listening**
> Country blues musicians: 'Blind' Lemon Jefferson, Lead Belly, Robert Johnson
> City blues musicians: B. B. King, Elmore James, Howlin' Wolf, T-Bone Walker

The Fifties

Doo-wop

Doo-wop is a style of vocal R&B music using nonsense syllables that originated in the late 1930s with the music of the Ink Spots. The name 'doo-wop' comes from a common phrase used in the backing vocals. Built on vocal harmony, it was popular with *a cappella* singing groups such as The Platters and The Coasters in the 1950s. The classic chord progression associated with doo-wop is I–VI–IV–V (C–Am–F–G in the key of C).

Rockabilly

Rockabilly was an early style of rock 'n' roll (see below) that became popular in the 1950s in the Southern States of America. It blended the sound of American country music with R&B (hence the name 'rockabilly', which melds the words 'rock' and 'hillbilly'). The sound is characterised by rhythmic drive, vocal twangs and tape echo. It can be heard in songs by Carl Perkins, Bill Haley and early Elvis Presley. Rockabilly enjoyed a revival during the 1970s and '80s with bands such as the Stray Cats.

Skiffle

Skiffle emerged in the UK in the mid-1950s and had its roots in trad. jazz and country music. Skiffle groups based their instrumentation around guitar, double bass and washboard, along with other homemade instruments. The leading skiffle performer of the time was banjoist Lonnie Donegan, whose single 'Rock Island Line' (1955) encouraged thousands of teenagers to create groups with acoustic guitars and home-made instruments.

Rock 'n' roll

Rock 'n' roll emerged in the USA during the 1950s. Its origins are in American blues, R&B and country. Bill Haley & the Comets' song 'Rock Around The Clock' brought rock 'n' roll music to the masses when it was featured in the 1956 film of the same name: it had a far-reaching effect on its audience and soon became a symbol of teenage rebellion. 'Rocket 88' (1951) by Jackie Brenston is often cited as the first rock 'n' roll song.

The song structure of rock 'n' roll music is often closely derived from the 12-bar blues. Key features of rock 'n' roll songs are:
- driving rhythms with a strong backbeat
- use of chords I, IV and V
- simple horn-section riffs in the same rhythm as the guitar
- a percussive walking bass

- a characteristic drum sound with a continuous rhythm on the rim of the snare drum, marked with big accents on the full head of the drum
- a 'chromatic blues turnaround' to finish.

> **Listening**
> US: Bill Haley & the Comets, Carl Perkins, Elvis Presley, Gene Vincent, Jerry Lee Lewis, Little Richard
> UK: Cliff Richard's 'Move it' (1958), Johnny Kidd & the Pirates' 'Shakin' All Over' (1960)

The Sixties

The 1960s was a decade of creativity and innovation, and many new styles of pop music developed in the aftermath of rock 'n' roll.

Soul

Soul music is a style of black American music that had its heyday during the sixties. The music is characterised by:
- gospel-influenced vocals with lyrical, soulful melodies
- an emphasis on the rhythm section
- large horn sections (trumpets, saxophones and trombones).

The most famous soul record labels were Stax, Atlantic and Tamla Motown, an all-black record company set up by Berry Gordy in Detroit.

- Tamla Motown records had a distinct sound and were all irresistibly danceable. The label's studio musicians included a string orchestra, and drums were supplemented with hand-claps or tambourine.
- Stax had its own house band – Booker T and the MGs. The Stax sound tended to be more raw and emotional, with closer links to gospel and blues, and leaving space for improvisation.

> **Listening**
> Aretha Franklin, Minnie Ripperton, Dionne Warwick
> Tamla Motown: Diana Ross and the Supremes, The Four Tops, Smokey Robinson and the Miracles, Marvin Gaye, Martha and the Vandellas, the Temptations
> Stax: Booker T and the MGs, Otis Redding, Wilson Pickett

British R&B

The term 'R&B' originally came into vogue when the American music magazine *Billboard* used it to describe a style of black American music that emerged in the 1940s and combined jazz and blues. It was designed to replace the expression 'race records', which had been used to describe African-American music. During the 1960s the style was adopted by British R&B groups who reinterpreted black American blues and gospel R&B. Many musicians who were part of the British R&B scene became prominent figures in the rock groups of the late sixties; leading the way were John Mayall, Alexis Korner and Eric Clapton.

1960s British beat music

Many British pop groups were heavily influenced by American blues and R&B, including the Beatles and the Rolling Stones. The Beatles helped to reshape Western pop music and were the most successful band ever. Every album was a huge hit, from the early material on *Please Please Me* (1961) to the hugely innovative *Sgt. Pepper's Lonely Hearts Club Band* (1967).

The Beatles had a distinct sound that used:
- British (rather than American) accents
- standard song forms
- distinctive chord sequences and vocal harmonies
- rhythmic guitar work
- simple melodies and clever lyrics.

Groups such as the Kinks, the Small Faces and The Who also helped to establish a British tradition that was characterised by:
- a guitar-driven pop style
- a classic line-up of lead guitar, bass guitar, drums and vocals
- verse and chorus structure, rich in hooks and with plenty of melodic interest
- conventional chord sequences.

> **Listening** The Beatles, The Kinks, The Rolling Stones, the Small Faces, the Searchers, The Who

The Seventies

Philly soul

Philly soul was an offshoot of 1960s soul that emerged in Philadelphia in the early 1970s. It was notable for its lavish productions that included lush string arrangements, close harmony and soulful vocals.

> **Listening** Harold Melvin & the Blue Notes, The O'Jays, The Three Degrees

Funk

Funk was a derivative of 1960s soul music; it had a grittier, harder sound that gave the bass, guitar and drums more prominence and made little or no use of orchestral backings. One of funk's earliest and most famous proponents was James Brown.

Funk is characterised by:
- a jazzy, raucous and energetic style
- guitar-driven music with punchy horns
- driving, sometimes Latin-American, syncopated rhythms
- groove-based parts (long sections with the same rhythms)
- repetitive, clipped riffs
- use of blue notes and jazz chords.

Listening Sly and the Family Stone, Funkadelic, Parliament and James Brown.

Disco

Disco was born in New York's discotheques – clubs that catered mostly to a black or gay clientele and focused on dancing. The sound was rooted in Philly soul and the grooves of funk. One of the most celebrated partnerships in disco was that of American singer Donna Summer and Italian producer Giorgio Moroder. Summer was the first disco star, with her 1975 hit 'Love To Love You Baby'; the 17-minute version, with its sexually charged vocals and sweeping, luxuriant strings, was a big hit in the clubs. Disco's uplifting music soon found a wider audience following the release of the 1977 film *Saturday Night Fever*.

Disco is a type of up-tempo dance music that combines:
- four-on-the-floor rhythms
- guitar-driven energy
- luscious orchestral arrangements of soul
- escapist lyrics about dancing, love and sex.

Donna Summer's disco song 'I Feel Love' (1977) was the first hit song to have an entirely synthesized backing track.

Listening The Bee Gees, Chic, KC and the Sunshine Band, Donna Summer

Music in Jamaica

Ska and rocksteady

1960s Jamaican music had a big influence on mainstream pop music. **Ska** fused the jazzy horns of American R&B with the rhythms of mento (Jamaica's calypso-style folk music). The music was often played through large, home-made sound systems; DJs would talk over the sounds, 'toasting' and speaking in rhythm with the music. Sound systems were an important development in Jamaican music and later gave rise to other musical offshoots such as rap, scratching and dance music. **Rocksteady** developed in the late 1960s; slower than ska, the jazzy horn lines gave way to a more prominent bass.

Characteristics
Ska
- electric guitars and a jazzy horn section
- fast tempo, with characteristic off-beat jumpy rhythms and jerky off-beat quavers

Rocksteady
- more relaxed rhythms
- rhythm guitar or keyboards
- stresses on beats 2 and 4
- loud bass guitar playing steady $\frac{4}{4}$ beat
- soulful singing
- lyrics with political themes

Listening
Ska: Jimmy Cliff, Prince Buster, Skatalites, The Specials (ska revival)
Rocksteady: Desmond Dekker and the Aces, Marcia Griffiths, Prince Buster

Reggae

Jamaica became independent in 1962 and people flocked into Kingston to seek work, settling in shanty towns such as Trench Town. There was high unemployment and a sense of protest that came to be voiced through reggae. Another reggae theme was Rastafarianism: a religion standing strong against the evil forces of Babylon and looking towards a return to Africa. Rastafarians regard Haile Selassie as their spiritual leader and advocate the use of ganja (cannabis) and the wearing of dreadlocks. The most famous Rastafarian, Bob Marley, became a spokesman for millions of young blacks. Musically, reggae was a direct descendant of ska and rocksteady.

Characteristics

- drums, bass and guitar play a repetitive accompaniment to the vocals
- off-beat bass drum, often reinforced by rim shots on the snare drum
- repeated off-beat quaver clipped guitar chords
- repeated four-bar bass pattern throughout
- lyrics with Rastafarian themes
- simple harmonies with few chord changes

Jamaican dub is a style of reggae in which new instrumental versions of songs are made by remixing existing recordings and adding effects such as echo and reverb. Dub artists and producers include Lee Scratch Perry. This was the beginning of remixing as a distinct art, and the dub effect of DJs talking over music led to the roots of rap (see page 139).

Listening Bob Marley and the Wailers, Delroy Washington, the Mighty Diamonds, Toots and the Maytals, U Roy

Heavy metal

With its roots in the British blues movement, the music of bands such as Deep Purple and Led Zeppelin took on a tougher, macho personality. First dubbed as 'hard rock' or 'heavy rock', heavy metal was built on high volume and electric guitar distortion.

Characteristics:
- screaming vocals
- driving rhythms
- high-decibel, fast distorted guitar solos, often using unison pentatonic riffs
- lyrics with sexual overtones or based on fantasy tales

Listening Led Zeppelin, Black Sabbath, Deep Purple

Folk rock

Folk clubs were still going strong in the UK in the sixties and, towards the end of the decade, folk rock emerged, introducing traditional songs into the pop repertoire.

Characteristics:
- UK folk rock combined traditional folk instruments (e.g. violin, mandolin) with the amplification and drum kits of rock.
- US folk rock focused on singer–songwriters, who sang reflective songs about their personal experiences accompanied by acoustic guitar.

> **Listening** Bob Dylan, Fairport Convention, James Taylor, John Martyn, Joni Mitchell

Jazz rock

Jazz rock is a blanket term used to cover various types of music that fuse elements of jazz and rock. On albums such as *Bitches Brew*, jazz trumpeter Miles Davis fuses the complexity and improvisation of jazz with elements of rock style. Jazz rock band Weather Report combined elements of free modal jazz, rock, funk and world music.

> **Listening** Blood, Sweat and Tears, Herbie Hancock, Miles Davis, Weather Report

Progressive (prog) rock

Progressive rock looked beyond the boundaries of rock in an attempt to elevate rock music onto a higher intellectual plane. It married poetic lyrics with electronic sounds, jazz and experimental rock. This style was album-based, with large-scale compositions and extended, often improvised, solos. Many albums were concept-based, telling epic stories or embracing over-arching themes.

> **Listening** Emerson, Lake and Palmer, King Crimson, Pink Floyd, Soft Machine, Yes

Glam rock

Glam rock emerged in the early seventies as a reaction against the serious aspirations of late-sixties rock music. Musically it was simple and catchy – what mattered more was the image: glitter, sequins and platform soles, make-up and an androgynous sexuality. Loosely speaking, there were two types of UK glam rock. The disposable music of bands such as Sweet and T Rex – sometimes known as 'glitter bands' – formed one type. But there was another, more esoteric, side to the movement, in which artists such as early glam pioneers David Bowie and Roxy Music appealed to a more sophisticated audience. The emphasis here was still on style, which applied to every aspect of their image, but the music was more ambitious. Glam rock was largely a British phenomenon, though it was represented by US bands New York Dolls and Kiss, with their highly theatrical outfits and concerts.

> **Listening** David Bowie, New York Dolls, Roxy Music, Sweet, Suzi Quatro, T Rex

Punk

Punk emerged in London during the late seventies. It was anti-establishment, anti-everything: a form of rebellion against unemployment. In part, it was a reaction against the virtuoso musicians and lengthy 'concept' albums produced by the arena rock bands. Although it was a British phenomenon, punk was influenced by US artists such as the New York Dolls and the Ramones, the latter laying down a musical blueprint with their simple chord progressions and catchy tunes played at blinding speed. In 1976 the Sex Pistols, under the management of Malcolm McClaren, were the first punk band to make their mark.

Punk music had a D.I.Y. 'anyone can do it' ethos. A typical line-up had a singer, two guitars and drums. Lyrics were often confrontational and were delivered in vernacular British, often London accents. The sound is characterised by:

- short, fast, highly aggressive songs using simple chord progressions
- aggressive, distorted guitars creating an impenetrable wall of sound
- a unique singing style, harsh and belligerent – a sort of sneering, recitative sound falling somewhere between singing, talking and shouting

> **Listening** The Clash, The Damned, Dead Kennedys, the Ramones, Sex Pistols

New Wave

In the aftermath of punk came New Wave. A hybrid of punk and pop, it took the vitality and powerful energy of punk, but rejected the nihilistic attitude. Though short, songs were more polished and the musicians more skilled. It was a diverse movement with bands ranging from The Jam – whose sound used aggressive guitars and political lyrics alongside the highly melodic vocals of Paul Weller – to the pop songs of Blondie.

> **Listening** Blondie, Elvis Costello and the Attractions, The Jam, B-52s, The Police, Talking Heads, the Undertones

The Eighties

New Romantic

The New Romantics emerged in the early eighties, owing much to the London club scene (Billy's and the Blitz). The New Romantic sound combined New Wave and synth pop with a more traditional 'straight' pop sound. The look was high on style and theatrical excess – something that was taken to extremes by heavily made-up, cross-dressing Boy George (of the band Culture Club). New Romantic band Duran Duran was one of the first acts to exploit the music video as a marketing tool.

Characteristics:
- elements of New Wave and synth pop
- slick, cleanly produced music
- synthesizers and pop guitars
- use of videos

> **Listening**   Culture Club, Duran Duran, Human League, Marilyn, Soft Cell, Spandau Ballet

Goth

In the late eighties, Goth began as a subgenre of punk, but soon the chain-saw guitar sound, aggressive rock drumming and anger-laden vocals were replaced by a more conventional, rock-oriented style with angular guitars, tom-heavy drums and doom-laden vocals. The Cure song 'A Forest' typifies the Goth sound, with its chorused, brooding guitars and anguished vocals. The Sisters of Mercy, with their motorbike jackets and dyed black hair, cultivated a dark, brooding edge; they used a drum machine in place of a drummer, setting a precedent for many Goth bands to follow.

Characteristics:
- crashing chords
- heavy bass lines
- low-pitched, doom-laden vocals
- nightmarish lyrics influenced by horror literature and the occult

> **Listening**   Bauhaus, The Cure, The Mission, Nick Cave and the Bad Seeds, Sisters of Mercy

Electro

In the eighties, when music technology prices fell and new instruments, such as programmable drum machines, became available, a new genre emerged that was later named electro. The roots of electro go back to the seventies, when Cabaret Voltaire used tape loops and experimental techniques to produce their individual sound. However, the biggest influence was the German band Kraftwerk, who eschewed guitars in favour of synthesizers and often treated the vocals with a Vocoder to produce a robotic, more synthetic sound. The dehumanized style influenced 1980s bands such as Ultravox and Tubeway Army, whose sound gradually became more reliant on synthesizers and electronic percussion. Tubeway Army's outlandish image and cold, detached lyrics proved to be a commercial success and the band had a big UK hit in 1979 with 'Are "Friends" Electric?'

Electro rarely uses syncopation but often uses:
• robotic vocals
• synthesizer keyboards and drum machines
• keyboards with octaves in the left hand
• minor keys.

Listening Depeche Mode, Kraftwerk, Human League, Orchestral Manoeuvres in the Dark, Pet Shop Boys, Soft Cell, Tubeway Army, Ultravox

Thrash metal

Thrash metal, an offshoot of heavy metal, developed in the 1980s, mainly hailing from the US West Coast (Metallica, Slayer) and New York (Anthrax). It featured extreme changes of tempo, with the fast sections being played as fast as possible, and dense, doubled-tracked guitars. The playing is often virtuosic. A punk influence can sometimes be felt in the belligerent sound and quasi-punk attitude; in turn the influence of thrash metal on the nu-metal movement of the late nineties and early noughties can be heard in the dense textures and high degree of technical proficiency.

Listening Anthrax, Metallica, Megadeth, Slayer

The Nineties

Hip-hop

Hip-hop originated in the Bronx area of New York in the seventies. Its vocal origins lie in the Jamaican 'toasting' tradition: black DJs such as Grandmaster Flash and the Jamaican-born 'father of hip-hop' Kool Herc extended the instrumental sections (or 'breaks') from records by mixing between two identical copies of the same record. Some of the DJs (or MCs) rapped over the top of the breaks. Dancers would get up during the breaks and perform a highly gymnastic style of dance using head and back-spinning. They became known as breakdancers.

The term 'hip-hop' refers to US urban black culture featuring DJ-ing, graffiti art, breakdancing, MC-ing and rap. Hip-hop music focuses on rhythm rather than melody and harmony. It is characterised by:
- rapping
- use of samples
- use of programmed beats
- DJ-ing.

> **Listening** Grandmaster Flash, Kool Herc, Public Enemy, Melle Mel, Sugar Hill Gang

R 'n' B

R 'n' B emerged in America during the late eighties through artists such as Janet Jackson and Whitney Houston. It is sometimes known as urban R 'n' B and is not to be confused with earlier R&B (see page 125).

R 'n' B combines elements of soul and hip-hop. It often uses:
- tight drum programming
- disco-influenced string sounds
- slick production techniques
- lush vocal arrangements, often with close harmonies
- hip-hop influences
- soul-influenced acrobatic vocals that are often semi-improvised, melismatic and virtuosic.

> **Listening** Whitney Houston, Mariah Carey, Destiny's Child, Beyoncé

Grunge

Generally centred around Seattle in America's North West, 'grunge' was a combination of early-seventies heavy rock and punk (although without punk's political agenda). Bands like Mudhoney and Nirvana took the bare basics of metal and added an element of punk attitude and aggression. Nirvana's best-selling album *Nevermind* included the grunge anthem 'Smells Like Teen Spirit'.

Grunge's defining characteristics are:
- the use of heavily distorted, fuzzy guitar
- heavy 'riffing'
- riffs played by a single guitar before being repeated by the whole band
- quiet verses building up to powerful choruses.

Listening Nirvana, Mudhoney, Pearl Jam, Pixies, Sonic Youth

Madchester

The 'Madchester' scene refers to a loose conglomeration of Manchester-based bands, some of whom had introduced elements of the newly arrived dance scene into their sound. A focal point of the scene was the Haçienda club, one of the first major clubs to play house music outside London. It was essentially a hybrid of dance and indie, and the influence of the emerging house scene can be heard in the hypnotically repetitive groove of the Happy Mondays' song 'Wrote For Luck' (1988).

Madchester music fused acid house dance rhythms with pop. It:
- often introduced elements of house music
- was influenced by the music of the sixties, particularly Beatles psychedelia
- featured sixties-sounding jangly guitars
- contained hooks in the choruses
- had dreamy reverb-laden vocals.

Listening Happy Mondays, Inspiral Carpets, Stone Roses

Britpop

Britpop was a move away from the electronic dance music and American 'grunge' of the nineties. Instead it looked back to the sixties for inspiration, including such British groups as the Kinks, The Who, the Small Faces and the Beatles. Britpop bands were also influenced by the Smiths, the Stone Roses and Happy Mondays, who all hailed from Manchester in the eighties and nineties (see 'Madchester', above).

Britpop music is characterised by:
- guitar-driven songs
- its classic line-up of lead guitar, bass guitar, drums and vocals
- verse and chorus structures
- strong melodies
- conventional chord sequences.

> **Listening** Blur, Oasis, Pulp, Suede

The 2000s

The noughties saw a fragmentation of styles, but few new genres outside of dance music.

Grime

Grime is a style of British music that emerged in the early 2000s. The main proponents of early grime were the members of the grime crews Roll Deep and Ruff Sqwad. In 2003 it was propelled into the mainstream when Dizzee Rascal's 'Boy In Da Corner' was released to wide critical acclaim. Grime draws on both hip-hop and dancehall, with most tracks featuring MCs.

Grime is characterised by:
- high-energy MC-ing
- sporadic bass stabs over syncopated broken beats and disjointed rhythms
- synth and percussion sounds that are often left raw, without further effects or processing.

> **Listening** Dizzee Rascal, Ruff Sqwad, So Solid Crew, Tinchy Stryder

Dance music from the 1980s to the present day

The roots of dance music are in Jamaican dub, funk, disco and electro-pop. It is a technology-based style in which DJs play an important role mixing and presenting tracks. The emphasis is on rhythm and timbre rather than melody and harmony.

Dance music is characterised by:
* extensive use of samples and loops
* new technology
* a layered texture made up of repeating motifs, rhythms or samples.

In the 1980s technology opened up different ways of creating music. The first two dance styles to emerge were **house** and **techno**.

House takes its name from Chicago's Warehouse club where, in the 1980s, DJ Frankie Knuckles manipulated recordings by lengthening some sections and repeating others. He also added pre-set percussion patterns to emphasise the solid beats – something that was soon to define house music. The short, repeating patterns of house music were facilitated by the technology available, which initially did not allow for long patterns to be programmed.

The origins of **techno** can be traced back to late-seventies Detroit, where DJ 'Electrifying Mojo' played an eclectic selection of music on his radio show, combining black funk alongside white electronica. This inspired three black high-school friends who became known as the 'Belleville Three' to invent the sound known as 'Detroit techno'.

Dance-music DJs use different ways to manipulate the sound of recordings, adding their own creative element to the music they play. DJs use vinyl records, CD decks, laptops and software packages to cut up tracks, loop sections and add new parts as part of a live performance. DJ techniques include mixing, scratching, beat matching, pitch-shifting, cueing and looping. There are many different styles of dance music, and these are being added to all of the time. The table on the following pages outlines the defining characteristics of some of the main dance styles.

Big beat

bpm 100–140

Characteristics
• A heavily sample-derived combination of loud compressed breakbeats and bass lines.

Listening Chemical Brothers, Fatboy Slim, Prodigy

Dubstep

bpm around 135–140

Characteristics
• Typified by its use of sub-bass, particularly 'wobble bass', often with the snare sounding on the third beat.
• Patterns are usually syncopated and are often swung.
• Much use of bass drop.
• Often uses minor keys and dissonant harmony.
• Variants include 'brostep', which takes the focus away from the sub-bass and places more emphasis on the mid-range, using layered synthesizers and extensive filtering to create wild textures.

Listening Crissy Criss, Skream

Electro house

bpm 120–130

Characteristics
• Layered synth parts, squeaks and bleeps, combined with a four on the floor drum beat and a resonant analogue bass riff. The many offshoots include fidget house with its short vocal samples, big synth stabs and pitch-bent bass lines.

Listening Benny Benassi, Bodyrox, Tocadisco

Hardcore

bpm 120–145

Characteristics
• A frenetically intense offshoot of acid house, with speeded-up drum loops and extensive use of breakbeats and samples.

Listening DJ Trax, Goldie, Prodigy

continues

Dance style characteristics

House

bpm around 120

Characteristics
• Originated in Chicago.
• Uses four on the floor bass drum, off-beat hi-hat patterns, samples and repetitive synthesizer riffs.
• Sometimes includes piano chords and vocals that are often soul-influenced.
• Variants include Piano House, which uses the bouncy piano riffs and block chords of the early Chicago days; and Deep House, which fuses elements of Chicago house with jazz-funk and often uses soulful vocals.

Listening Basement Jaxx, Farley Jackmaster Funk, Marshal Jefferson, Todd Terry

Jungle/drum'n bass

bpm around 170

Characteristics
• Often contains little more than a drum loop and a heavy bass line, hence the name.
• Uses speeded-up hip-hop breaks and high-speed retriggering of the drums.
• Live drum'n bass uses electric, electronic and acoustic instruments, along with MC-ing.

Listening Andy C, Calyx & TeeBee, DJ Hazard, Goldie, Roni Size, Shy FX, Dilinja

Rap/hip-hop

bpm 90–110

Characteristics
• Originally based on loops of seventies funk and disco, often programmed beats are used.
• Focuses on rhythm rather than melody and harmony.
• Accompanied by a rhythmic 'rap' vocal.
• Offshoots include gangsta rap and West Coast rap.

Listening Eminem, Jay-Z, J Dilla, N.W.A., Kanye West

continues

Garage

bpm around 120

Characteristics
- Combines house loops with time-stretched vocals and deep synthesized bass lines derived from drum'n bass.
- Often uses synth string sections.
- Variants include the faster 'bass-line house' with its heavy bass line, pitched-up vocals and grime-style MC-ing four on the floor drum beat.

Listening Double 99, Mis-Teeq, T2 and Jodie Aysha

Techno

bpm 120–140

Characteristics
- Originated in Detroit.
- Has similar drum patterns to house, but heavily electronic with more use of purely synthetic sounds and short repeated phrases.
- Early tracks often had little or no chord movement.
- Variants include Detroit techno and acid techno.

Listening DJ Misjah and DJ Tim, Plastikman, Nicholas Jaar

Trance

bpm 120–150

Characteristics
- An offshoot of techno, very synthesizer oriented, but with more emphasis on harmony.

Listening Faithless, William Orbit, Underworld

Trip-hop

bpm 60–100

Characteristics
- Mellow, heavily compressed sounds with a slow dreamy fusion of hip-hop breaks and experimental drum textures. Lo-Fi sound.

Listening Future Sound Of London, Massive Attack, Portishead, Smith and Mighty, Tricky

Appendix 1:
Table of scales and modes

Major scales

Natural minor scales

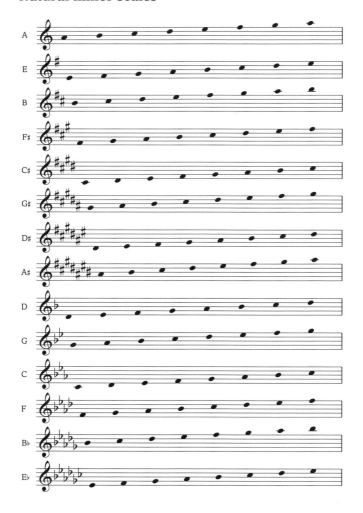

Harmonic minor scales

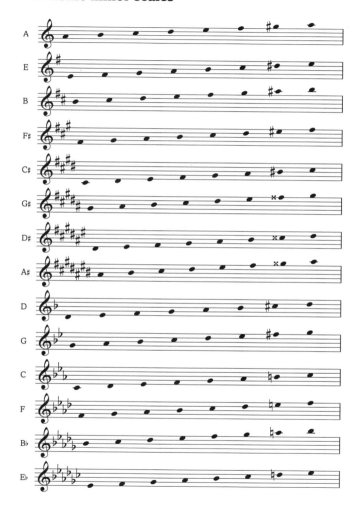

Melodic minor scales

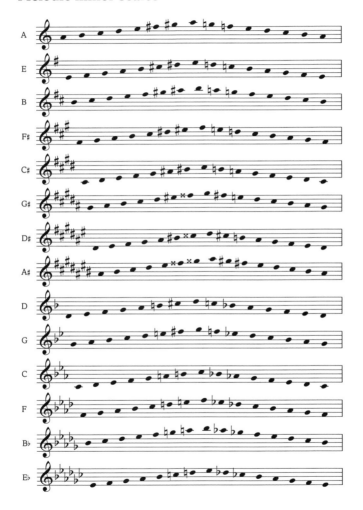

Main modes

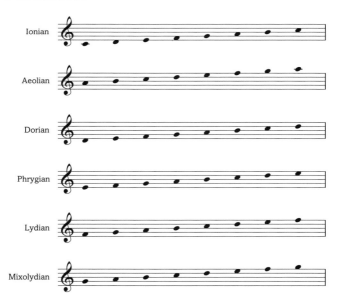

The blues scale

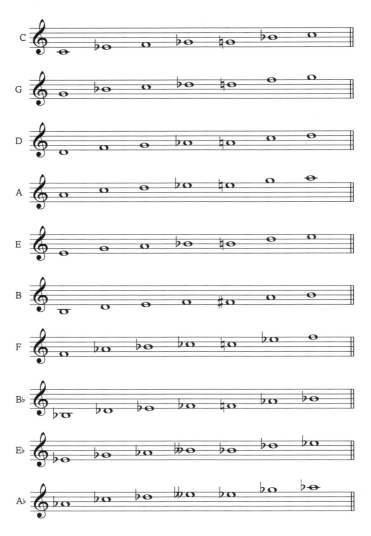

Appendix 2: Reading TAB notation

Guitar

Tablature (or TAB) notation is a graphic depiction of the six strings of the guitar, where each line represents a different string:

- The top line represents the top E string. This is the thinnest string (first string).
- The bottom line represents the bottom E string. This is the thickest string (sixth string).
- Numbers are placed on each string to indicate at which fret it should be pressed down. '0' means that you should play the open string; '1' means press down at the first fret, etc.
- If there is no number on a string, then that string should not be played.

In the example below, the bottom E string should be played on the 3rd fret:

A **chord** is indicated when the numbers are placed in a vertical line. In the following example, a C chord is shown:

An **arpeggiated chord** is indicated when the numbers are placed one after another. The following example shows an arpeggiated C chord:

> To play the first three notes, play: (1) the fifth string at the third fret, (2) the fourth string at the second fret and (3) the open third string.

Similarly, a **single-note line** is shown with the numbers placed one after another. Here is a scale of C:

When an alternative tuning is needed, this is usually shown at the top of the TAB. For instance: *Guitar tuning low–high E–B–E–G♯–B–E*

For the representation of specific guitar techniques such as bends and hammer-ons, see page 87.

Bass guitar

Tablature (or TAB) notation is also a graphic depiction of the four strings of the bass guitar, where each line represents a different string:

> If the TAB is for five-string bass then there will be five lines, and there will be six lines for a six-string bass.

- The top line represents the top G string. This is the thinnest string (first string).

- The bottom line represents the bottom E string. This is the thickest string (fourth string).

- Numbers are placed on each string to indicate at which fret the string should be pressed down. '0' means that you should play the open string; '1' means press down at the first fret, etc.

- If there is no number on a string, then that string should not be played.

In the example below, the bottom E string should be played on the 3rd fret:

A **single-note line** is shown with the numbers placed one after another. Here is a scale of C:

To play the first bar, play (1) the third string at the third fret, (2) the open second string, (3) the second string at the second fret and (4) the second string at the third fret.

When an alternative tuning is needed, this is usually shown at the top of the TAB. For instance: *tune E string down to E♭*

For the representation of specific guitar techniques, such as bends and hammer-ons, see page 87.

Appendix 3:
Reading drum notation

Clefs are not used in drum kit notation; instead, the lines and spaces of a standard five-lined stave represent different parts of the drum kit.

There is no universal method for notating music for drum kit, so it is useful to include a key to the various symbols; here is one of the most common methods:

| High tom | Mid tom | Snare drum | Floor tom | Bass drum (BD) |

In this method, the bass drum part is placed in the bottom space, the high tom in the top space, and so on.

Different note-heads and positions on the stave are used to denote other parts of the drum kit, and the different ways of playing them. In the example below, the hi-hat is shown by a ×, placed above the stave when played with sticks and below the stave when played with the foot.

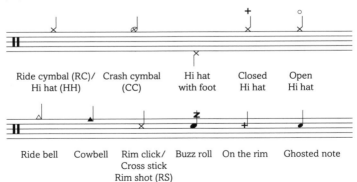

| Ride cymbal (RC)/ Hi hat (HH) | Crash cymbal (CC) | Hi hat with foot | Closed Hi hat | Open Hi hat |

| Ride bell | Cowbell | Rim click/ Cross stick Rim shot (RS) | Buzz roll | On the rim | Ghosted note |

Often drum and other percussion parts are made up of short repeated patterns. The sign ⅍ means repeat the previous bar.

The sign | ⅍ | means repeat the previous two bars:

Slash notation means continue in a similar style:

Glossary

8va To be performed an octave higher than written. Similarly 8vb should be performed an octave lower than written

12-bar blues A commonly used form made up of three four-bar phrases and built on three chords: the tonic, the subdominant and the dominant

32 bar song form Sometimes known as AABA, the form consists of four eight-bar phrases that are built on two melodic ideas ('A' and 'B')

a cappella Sung without an instrumental accompaniment

accent Accented notes should be played with emphasis and a short attack

accidental Each note can have its pitch slightly raised or lowered by the addition of an accidental. A sharp (♯), flat (♭) or natural (♮) is used to raise or lower the pitch of a note by a semitone

ad lib section A free section where the vocalist improvises passages that are usually based on earlier material

added 6th chord A chord where a 6th above the root is added to a major triad

Aeolian mode A mode following the pattern of intervals formed by A – B – C – D – E – F – G – A, the same pattern of tones and semitones as the natural minor scale

Amen cadence Another name for the plagal cadence (see plagal cadence)

anacrusis When a phrase begins on a weak beat, it is said to start with an anacrusis

arpeggio A type of broken chord in which the notes are played in order from the lowest to the highest or vice versa

articulation An indication of the precise way in which notes are to be performed, e.g. accented or legato (smoothly)

augmented chord A chord built up from the root plus a major 3rd plus an augmented 5th, e.g. C – E – G♯

backbeat The rhythmic emphasis on beats 2 and 4 within a four-beat bar. Many rock drum patterns are based around the kick (bass) drum played on beats 1 and 3 with the snare drum sounding the backbeat on beats 2 and 4

ballad A slow, usually romantic song with expressive vocals and melody

bars and bar-lines Music is divided up into bars (sometimes known as measures) that contain a specified number of beats. The bars are separated by bar-lines

bass drop Where a quiet section in dance music is followed by one that is loud and intense

beat The underlying pulse

beat matching A mixing technique used by DJs which involves changing the speed at which a record is played so that its tempo matches that of the song currently playing

bend Where the pitch of a note is changed slightly, usually raised

blue note A flattened note – commonly the 3rd, 5th or 7th of a major scale

blues scale A six-note scale using blue notes (commonly the flattened 3rd, 5th and 7th)

bpm Beats per minute

break Where most instruments stop playing, leaving one instrument (or singer) continuing alone, usually for one or two bars

breakbeat A repeated drum part in dance music, often sampled, sliced and manipulated

breakdown The section of a dance track where sounds drop out in order to create tension as they build up again

bridge See *middle eight*

broken chord When the notes of a chord are sounded individually

cadence Cadences are used to

punctuate music, either bringing a melody to a point of repose before going on, or bringing it to a close. Cadences are found at the end of musical phrases and are usually harmonised by two chords

call and response Where a soloist sings a phrase and a larger group responds with an answering phrase. It is often found in gospel-influenced soul and R&B

chord The simultaneous sounding of two or more notes to produce harmony

chord progression A repeated sequence of chords

chord sequence See *chord progression*

chorus 1. A setting of the refrain of the lyrics, often containing the title words of the song. The chorus usually returns several times, and is likely to be the 'catchiest' and loudest part of the song

2. A guitar effect sounding like many guitars playing at once

chromatic harmony Chromatic harmony uses notes from outside the key to colour the chords

chromatic scale A scale made up of all the twelve notes in an octave and formed entirely of semitones. It may begin on any note

circle of fifths 1. A series of chords whose roots are each a 5th lower than the previous chord, e.g. A – D – G – C

2. A circular diagram demonstrating the relationship between different keys

clef A sign written at the start of the stave telling you what pitches are being shown

close harmony When the intervals between two or more voices are close together

coda A concluding section

common time $\frac{4}{4}$ (four crotchet beats in a bar) – the most common time

signature. It is sometimes shown by a letter **C**

compound interval An interval wider than an octave

compound time Compound time signatures use a dotted note as the main beat; this is often a dotted crotchet, e.g. $\frac{6}{8}$ and $\frac{9}{8}$. In compound time, the dotted beat is divisible by three

concert pitch 1. A term used to distinguish between the written and sounding notes of a transposing instrument. A score at concert pitch is written in the key that the music sounds

2. The standard of pitch used for tuning instruments, 440 vibrations per second for A above middle C

consonance Consonant chords and intervals feel relatively stable

crescendo Getting louder

cueing Finding a suitable point on a record for the DJ to mix a new track in

decrescendo Getting quieter

diatonic 1. Pertaining to a major or minor scale

2. Using a major or minor key without chromatic alteration

diminished 7th chord A diminished triad plus a diminished 7th, e.g. C – Eb – Gb – Bbb

diminished chord A chord built up from the root plus a minor 3rd plus a diminished 5th

e.g. C – Eb –Gb

diminuendo Getting quieter

dissonance Dissonant chords and intervals feel somewhat unstable, as though one of the notes needs to move up or down to resolve into a consonance

dominant The fifth degree of a scale

dominant 7th chord A major triad plus a minor 7th built on the fifth degree of the scale, the dominant e.g. G – B – D – Bb

Dorian mode A mode following the pattern of intervals formed by D – E – F – G – A – B – C – D

double sharp/double flat Sometimes it is necessary to sharpen a note that has already been sharpened, or to flatten a note that has already been flattened. These notes are indicated by double sharp (♯♯) and double flat (♭♭) signs

duple time Two beats in a bar

duplet Where two notes are played in the time of three

dynamics Varying degrees of loudness and quietness at which music can be performed

enharmonic Notes that sound the same but are written (or 'spelt') differently are said to be enharmonic e.g. E♯ and F

enharmonic interval Where two intervals have different names but sound the same. The augmented 4th (e.g. C – F♯) and the diminished 5th (e.g. C – G♭) are enharmonic equivalents because the F♯ sounds the same as the G♭

extended chords Extended chords add further notes to seventh chords e.g. ninth, eleventh and thirteenth chords

falsetto The vocal register above the one a voice naturally speaks or sings in

fermata A fermata (pause sign) means that the note or rest should be prolonged

figuration Short repeated patterns of notes with a distinctive shape (e.g. scales or arpeggio patterns), often used as decoration or accompaniment

fill A short decorative embellishment of an otherwise repeating drum pattern, often used as 'punctuation', marking a change from one section to another

flat A flat (♭) placed before a note lowers its pitch by one semitone

forte/fortissimo Loud/very loud

four on the floor A bass-drum style often found in disco and EDM. The bass drum plays on all four beats of the $\frac{4}{4}$ bar

full-close Another name for a perfect cadence - the dominant chord followed by the tonic chord at the end of a phrase

full-score The written form of a musical composition including parts for all of the instruments

fuzz box A guitar effect with a fuzzy, distorted sound

G. P. A general pause where all performers are silent, usually for one or two bars

glissando A slide

groove A repeated rhythmic idea and 'feel'. It is often the main rhythm of a song and may run right through the track.

half close Another name for an imperfect cadence - almost any chord (but usually the tonic, supertonic or subdominant) followed by the dominant at the end of a phrase

harmony Harmony is produced when any combination of notes are sounded together

harmonics High-pitched notes with a different, 'silvery' sound quality. They are also known as 'overtones'

harmonic rhythm The rate at which chords change

hook A short catchy melodic idea designed to be easily memorable.

horn section The wind and brass section – most often saxophones and trumpets, also sometimes trombones

imperfect cadence Almost any chord (but usually the tonic, supertonic or subdominant) followed by the dominant at the end of a phrase

improvisation A performance where the music is made up on the spot. It is usually based on chords or melodic material

instrumental A section without the voice, often improvised, and usually based on the chords of the verse or chorus

intro The opening section of a song

interrupted cadence The dominant chord leads the listener to expect a perfect cadence at the end of a phrase, but instead of the expected tonic chord, another chord (often the submediant) is used

interval The distance between two notes. When two notes are played together they form a harmonic interval; when played separately, they form a melodic interval

inversion A chord is said to be in inversion when a note other than the root is the bass note. In pop music, chords in inversion are often known as slash chords

Ionian mode A mode following the pattern of intervals formed by C – D – E – F – G – A – B – C, the same pattern of tones and semitones as the major scale

key When a piece of music is based on a particular scale it is said to be in the key of that scale.

key signature A sign at the beginning of each stave of music indicating the key of the piece.

legato Smoothly

leading note The seventh degree of the scale

lead sheet A type of short score often including only the lyrics and chords. Some may also include the vocal line, tempo and feel, and any important melodic lines

lick A short solo

looping Where a short section or sample is repeated over and over again, often rhythmic in nature

Lydian mode A mode following the pattern of intervals formed by F – G – A – B – C – D – E – F.

major chord A chord built up from the root plus a major 3rd plus a perfect 5th e.g. C – E – G

major 7th chord A major triad plus a major 7th, e.g. C – E – G – B

mediant The third degree of a scale

melisma Where a group of notes is sung to one syllable

mezzo Moderately

middle C The C nearest the centre of the piano keyboard

middle eight A contrasting section (not necessarily eight bars long) in a song, often with a different arrangement of instruments, and/or different chords. Sometimes the middle eight is referred to as the bridge

minor chord A chord built up from the root plus a minor 3rd plus a perfect 5th e.g. C – E♭ –G

minor 7th chord A minor triad plus a minor 7th, e.g. C – E♭ – G – B♭

minor 7th flat 5 chord A diminished triad plus a minor 7th e.g. C – E♭ – G♭ – B♭

mix in The opening section of a dance track, where the DJ mixes the previous track into the new one

Mixolydian mode A mode following the pattern of intervals formed by G – A – B – C – D – E – F – G

mix out The closing section of a dance track, where the DJ starts to mix in the next track

mixing Where two tracks are mixed together. This is done through beat-matching and sometimes pitch control

modal Music based on a mode rather than a key

mode Modes are seven-note scales based on different consecutive series of 'white notes' found on a keyboard. Each mode has a unique pattern of intervals and may start on any note

modulation Key change

motif A short melodic or rhythmic idea

natural A natural (♮) restores a note, previously sharpened or flattened, to its original pitch

octatonic scale A scale is made up of eight notes alternating between tones and semitones

octave The interval between the first and last notes of a major or minor scale. The two notes have the same letter name

oral tradition Transmitted from one generation to another by word of mouth

outro The closing section of a song

overdrive A guitar effect produced by slightly distorting the signal

parallel chords Parallel chords keep the same shape from one chord to the next so that the lines move in parallel

pedal 1. A sustained or repeated note sounded against changing harmony 2. A device used by guitarists to produce effects

pentatonic scale A five-note scale

perfect cadence The dominant chord followed by the tonic chord at the end of a phrase

phaser A guitar effect producing a swirling sound

phrase A subdivision of a melodic line

Phrygian mode A mode following the pattern of intervals formed by E – F – G – A – B – C – D – E

piano/pianissimo Quiet/very quiet

pitch The word used to describe how high or low a sound is

pitch shifting
An effect used by DJs produced when changing the speed of a record

pivot chord A chord common to two keys that can be used to smooth out a key change, e.g. a G chord can act as a pivot chord when modulating from C major to D major

plagal cadence The subdominant chord followed by the tonic chord at the end of a phrase

power chord A chord used in rock music made up of just two pitches – the root and the 5th

pre-chorus A short transitional section leading into the chorus

primary triads The triads built upon the tonic, subdominant and dominant degrees of the scale

pulse The underlying beat in a piece of music

PVG A type of short score arranged for piano, vocals and guitar

quadruple time Four beats in a bar

quintuplet Five notes played in the time of four

range 1. The distance between the lowest and highest notes of a melody or composition
2. The distance between the lowest and highest notes that can be played by an instrument or sung by a vocalist

register A particular part of the range of a voice (e.g. chest or head voice) or instrument (e.g. high or low register)

rapping Rhythmical, rhyming, semi-spoken recitation

related keys Keys which have the most notes in common. The three most closely related keys are the dominant (V), the subdominant (IV) and the relative minor or major

relative major/minor Major and minor keys with the same key signatures are said to be related. C major is the relative major of A minor, and A minor is the relative minor of C major

riff A short, repeated melodic pattern that may be heard at different pitches to fit in with the harmony. It may also slightly change its shape

root The note that corresponds with the letter-name of the chord, e.g. the root of a chord of G is always G regardless of whether it is the bass note of the chord

root position A chord arranged with the root as the bass note

sample A digitally recorded fragment of sound, newly recorded or from a pre-existing source

scale A pattern of notes arranged in order, from low to high (or vice versa)

scat Singing using nonsense syllables

score The written form of a musical composition

scratching Moving a vinyl record back and forth as it is playing creating a rhythmic percussive sound

secondary chords (or triads) Chords built on the 2nd, 3rd, 6th and 7th degrees of the scale are known as secondary triads i.e. the supertonic, mediant, submediant and leading note

semitone A semitone is a measurement of pitch. There are semitones between all adjacent notes on a keyboard, whether black or white

septuplet Seven notes played in the time of four

seventh chord Seventh chords are made by adding a 7th above the root on top of a triad

sextuplet Six notes played in the time of four

sharp A sharp (♯) placed before a note raises its pitch by one semitone

short score A type of written form of a musical composition including only the most important elements, e.g. a lead sheet or a PVG

simple interval An interval of an octave or less

simple time Simple time signatures use an un-dotted note as the main beat e.g. $\frac{4}{4}$ or $\frac{2}{2}$. In simple time the beats are divisible into halves

slash chord A chord in inversion where the bass note is indicated by a slash and the letter name of the bass note after the letter name of the root, e.g. C/G

slur Slurs (⌣) are used to link two or more consecutive notes together. Slurred notes should be played smoothly

split common time $\frac{2}{2}$ (two minim beats in a bar). It is sometimes shown by (split common time sign)

stab A single accented chord

staccato Staccato notes should be played lightly, short and detached

staff or stave A set of five parallel lines with four spaces between them. Sounds of different pitches are placed on the lines or in the spaces: the higher up the stave, the higher the pitch

subdominant The fourth degree of a scale

submediant The sixth degree of a scale

substitution chords Interchangeable chords – where one chord can be substituted for a similar chord within a chord progression

supertonic The second degree of a scale

suspended chord In suspended chords (or sus chords) the 3rd of a major or minor chord is replaced by the 2nd or the 4th. The sound is neither major nor minor

swung rhythm In each pair of notes, the first is played a little longer than the second. Pairs of quavers in $\frac{4}{4}$, for instance, typically sound like a lazy $\frac{12}{8}$ when swung

syncopation The effect created when off-beat notes are accented

TAB (tablature) notation A way of writing music for guitar or bass where each line represents a different string

tempo The speed of a piece of music

tenuto Tenuto notes should be slightly stressed and then held on for their full value:

texture The relationship between simultaneously sounding lines in a piece of music, e.g. the number of layers, the use of chords or single notes

three-chord trick The practice of building a song on the three primary triads – tonic, subdominant and dominant

tie A curved line joining two or notes of the same pitch together. The note values are added together to make one longer sustained note

timbre Tone colour, quality of sound

time signature A numerical sign found at the beginning of a piece of music telling you the number of beats in each bar and the note-value of the beat

toasting A cross between talking and rhythmic chanting originally practised by Jamaican MCs

tonality The key centre or mode of a piece of music

tone 1. A measurement of pitch made up of two semitones, e.g. C – D
2. The timbre of a particular instrument or voice

tonic The first degree of a major or minor scale, the key note

tonic major, tonic minor Two keys that share the same tonic, e.g. G major and G minor

transposition The process of writing or performing music at a higher or lower pitch than the original

tremolo Very fast continuous repetitions of individual or alternating notes

tremolo arm or whammy bar A guitar device used to produce a range of effects by raising and lowering the pitch of notes

triple time Three beats in a bar

triplet Where three notes are played in the time of two

turnaround The final part of a song section in which the melody or chords lead into the next section

unison Two voices producing the same pitch are said to be in unison

verse A section of a song which is repeated, each time with different words

verse and chorus A standard song form where the verse and chorus usually alternate

vibrato The regular, rapid fluctuation of pitch that can be used to add warmth to a note.

voicing How the individual notes within chords are arranged

wah-wah pedal A device which continuously varies the tone a guitar producing vowel-like sounds

walking bass A steady bass-line that 'walks' along, marking all four beats of the bar and usually mixing arpeggio and scale-type movement

whole-tone scale A scale made up of six consecutive whole tones

word painting Where the text of a song is reflected in the music

Index

Notes

Notes

Notes

Notes